THE BEST OF
GOOD
LIVING
WITH
Jane Asher

THE BEST OF
GOOD
LIVING
WITH
Jane Asher

CREATIVE IDEAS
FOR YOUR FAMILY
AND HOME

BBC BOOKS

This book has been published to accompany the
TV series *Good Living*, a BBC Manchester production.

Editor: Liz Warner
Series Producer: Ben Frow
Producers: Anna Beattie and Fiona Wright

Published by BBC Books, an imprint of
BBC Worldwide Ltd, Woodlands,
80 Wood Lane, London W12 0TT

First published in 1998

ISBN 0 563 38417 4

Edited by Bridget Hetzel
Designed by Janet James

Printed and bound in Great Britain
by Butler & Tanner Ltd, Frome & London
Colour separations by Radstock Reproductions Ltd,
Midsomer Norton
Jacket printed by Lawrence Allen Ltd,
Weston-super-Mare

Much of the material in this book has previously
been published in *Good Living with Jane Asher*,
a supplement to *BBC Good Food Magazine*.

contents

introduction

I've always enjoyed cooking, making crafts and experimenting with ideas for the house and garden, but, like everybody nowadays, I never seem to have time to do as much as I'd like. When I first got married I would spend hours in the kitchen slaving over a special meal and then spend the evening in a state of tension worrying whether it would all work, or I'd try to make some complicated handmade craft for a present and feel horribly guilty when I never managed to finish it. The accumulation of family and work commitments forced me to change, and I have become far more relaxed about entertaining and about making things for the house in general. *Good Living* is all about quick, effective and realistic ways to make life at home just that little bit more fun, and whether it's unusual flower arrangements, fast but delicious family meals, tips for simple make-overs, spectacular cakes, home-made crafts or recipes to surprise your guests, I know you'll find plenty of irresistible ideas in every chapter.

All the basic principles are easy to follow and many of the instructions can be adapted to suit exactly what you need. I've learnt a great deal and picked up some wonderful tips from the experts we've called on for *Good Living* and the best of their ideas are gathered here together with some of my own recipes and hints that I've developed during 25 years of looking after a home and family.

I'm sure you'll find many things to cook or make in the following pages that will bring you as much pleasure as they have me.

JANE ASHER

recipes to impress

All the recipes in this section look fantastic and taste even better. If you've been slaving away in the kitchen you deserve a little appreciation, and these beautiful ideas will make very impressive centrepieces on your table, or unusual gifts for your family and friends.

The French have always been excellent at producing delicate and elegant pâtisserie and they were our inspiration for making these simply delicious tarts. Our open tarts are made with various pastries: some are ready-made while others, such as the easy, pizza-like, dried-yeast dough for the Pissaladière, are made at home. But it is the scrumptious fillings that make these tarts so special – the vanilla custard in the Tartes aux pruneaux is wonderful, as are the caramelized apples in the Tarte Tatin.

french
tarts

Tartes aux pruneaux à la crème pâtissière

Traditionally these tarts are made with *quetsches*, the purple cooking plums from Alsace, but any plums with a good flavour will be delicious.

Makes 8

2 x 350g pkts fresh sweet shortcrust pastry

FOR THE VANILLA CUSTARD
125ml/4fl oz milk
150ml/¼ pint double cream
½ vanilla pod, split in half or 1 tsp natural vanilla essence
3 eggs
85g/3oz caster sugar, plus extra for dusting
1 tsp plain flour
16 plums, halved and stoned

1 Preheat the oven to 220C/425F/Gas 7. Roll out the pastry on a lightly floured surface, then use to line eight 12cm/4½ in loose-bottomed tart tins. Line with greaseproof paper, pile in some baking beans and bake blind for 6-8 minutes until the pastry is set, but not golden. Remove pastry cases from the oven, then reduce the oven temperature to 200C/400F/Gas 6.
2 Make the vanilla custard: heat the milk and cream with the vanilla until boiling, then remove from the heat. Remove the vanilla pod, if using, and scrape the tiny black seeds into the custard. Whisk the eggs and the sugar together, whisk in the flour, then very gradually beat in the hot vanilla cream.
3 Remove the baking beans and greaseproof paper from the pastry cases and arrange four plum halves in each tart. If your plums are very juicy, place skin-side down to prevent the pastry from becoming too soggy.
4 Pour over the vanilla custard, then bake for 15 minutes or until the custard is set and just starting to turn golden. Cool slightly, and carefully remove from the tins. Dust with caster sugar and serve warm.

Tarte au citron et aux amandes

This lemon tart from Provence has a wonderful texture. The filling is dense and almondy while the pastry is almost cake-like. For an added twist, we've included a hint of lavender.

Serves 8-10

FOR THE PASTRY

2 eggs, beaten
100g/3¹/₂ oz caster sugar
200g/7oz self-raising flour
115g/4oz butter, diced

FOR THE ALMOND FILLING

3 eggs
140g/5oz caster sugar
grated rind and juice 2 lemons
140g/5oz unsalted butter, softened
85g/3oz ground almonds
2 tbsp plain flour
12 blanched almond halves
petals from 3 fresh or dried lavender flowers
icing sugar and fresh lavender, to decorate
  (optional)

1 Make the pastry: place the eggs and sugar in a food processor and blend until well mixed. Gradually add the flour to make a paste, then add the butter and blend again until it is incorporated. The mixture will be extremely soft, more like a cake mixture, but don't worry. Wrap in plastic film, then chill for at least 3 hours, preferably overnight, until it is firm enough to roll out.

2 Preheat the oven to 200C/400F/Gas 6. Roll out the pastry on a lightly floured surface, then working very quickly use to line a 26cm/10¹/₂ in loose-bottomed fluted flan tin.

3 Prick the pastry with a fork and line the pastry case with greaseproof paper. Fill with baking beans and bake blind for 15 minutes until the pastry is set and just starting to brown. Remove the tart from the oven and reduce the oven temperature to 190C/375F/Gas 5. Carefully remove the baking beans and greaseproof paper and press the pastry back to the shape of the tin if it has risen unevenly while baking.

4 Make the filling: whisk the eggs and sugar together, then beat in the lemon rind and juice, butter, ground almonds and flour. Pour into the pastry case, then top with the blanched almonds and scatter with the lavender petals.

5 Bake for 25-30 minutes or until the filling is firm and golden. Cool slightly, then remove from the tin. Serve warm, dusted with icing sugar and more lavender petals, if liked.

Tarte Tatin avec de la crème Calvados

Here is a real French classic, invented, reportedly by mistake, by the Tatin sisters in the 1850s when one of them inadvertently put the apples she had cooked in butter and sugar in a tart tin without a pastry lining. Instead of tipping the apples out, she placed the pastry on top, then turned the tart upside down after baking. In this version, for an autumn feeling, we've added blackberries.

Serves 6

FOR THE PASTRY

225g/8oz plain flour
85g/3oz caster sugar
115g/4oz butter, softened
1 egg, beaten

FOR THE CARAMELIZED APPLES

85g/3oz unsalted butter
175g/6oz caster sugar
1kg/2¼lb firm eating apples such as Braeburn,
*   peeled, quartered and cored*
juice of 2 lemons
115g/4oz large blackberries

FOR THE CALVADOS CREAM

300ml/½ pint double cream
2 tbsp Calvados
2 tbsp icing sugar, sifted

1 Make the pastry: tip the flour and sugar into a food processor, then add the butter and blend until the mixture resembles crumbs. Add the egg and blend again to make a soft dough. Wrap in plastic film, then chill for at least 1 hour.
2 Preheat the oven to 220C/425F/Gas 7. Grease the base of a non-stick round 23cm/9in cake tin (not a loose-bottomed one).
3 Cook the caramelized apples: melt the butter in a large non-stick frying pan, then add the sugar and stir over a fairly high heat until the mixture turns to a golden caramel. Add the apples and lemon juice and continue cooking and stirring for 10 minutes or until the apples have softened but still hold their shape. Tip the apples and caramel into the tin in an even layer, then scatter over the blackberries.
4 Roll out the pastry on a lightly floured surface so that it is slightly larger than the tin and place over the apples and blackberries, tucking in the overlapping pastry. Bake for 25 minutes or until the pastry is golden.
5 Whip together the Calvados cream ingredients. Cool the tart in the tin for a few minutes. If necessary, slide a sharp knife around the tin edges to loosen slightly, then carefully invert on to a plate and serve with the cream.

Pissaladière

This is really a French version of a pizza, although the cheese-free topping is always the same – rich, caramelized onions, fragrant, fresh herbs, anchovies and olives.

Serves 4-6

FOR THE DOUGH

225g/8oz strong plain flour
2 tsp easy-blend yeast
1 tsp salt
1 tsp sugar
150ml/¼ pint warm water
1 tbsp olive oil

FOR THE FILLING

2 tbsp olive oil
6 large onions, thinly sliced
3 garlic cloves, finely chopped
2 bay leaves
2-3 tsp fresh thyme leaves
50g can anchovy fillets, drained and halved
  lengthways
10 pitted black olives
salt and freshly ground black pepper

1 Make the dough: mix the flour in a bowl with the yeast, salt and sugar, then stir in the warm water and oil to make a soft dough. Knead for a few minutes on an unfloured work surface until smooth, then place in an oiled plastic food bag. Seal very securely.
2 Immerse the bag in a large bowl of warm water and set aside for 30 minutes or until the dough has doubled in size.
3 Make the filling: heat the oil in a large non-stick frying pan. Fry the onions, garlic, bay leaves, half the thyme leaves and seasoning, stirring regularly, for 10-15 minutes until the onions are really soft and golden.
4 Preheat the oven to 220C/425F/Gas 7. Oil a 33 x 24cm/13 x 9½ in Swiss roll tin. Remove the dough

from the bag, but don't knead or it will become too elastic to shape – instead gently pull and flatten it to cover and go up the sides of the tin.
5 Spread the onion mixture evenly on top of the dough, then make a lattice pattern with the anchovies. Scatter over the olives and bake for 25 minutes until golden. Sprinkle with the remaining thyme and serve hot, warm or at room temperature.

Tartes aux tomates

These couldn't be simpler as they are made using a ready-rolled puff pastry sheet. For added flavour, you can spread the pastry with sun-dried tomato or olive paste before piling on the tomatoes.

Makes 4

375g ready-rolled puff pastry sheet,
  thawed if frozen
1 egg, beaten
2 tbsp olive oil
leaves from small pot fresh basil
6 large vine-ripened tomatoes, thickly sliced
salt and freshly ground black pepper

1 Preheat the oven to 220C/425F/Gas 7. Unravel the pastry then, using a saucer as a template, cut out four circles and place on a baking sheet. Brush the pastry circles with egg and bake for 8-10 minutes until golden.
2 Meanwhile, place the oil and three-quarters of the basil leaves in a food processor with seasoning and blend until the basil is very finely chopped.
3 Press the puff pastry circles down to flatten, then spoon over a little of the basil oil and sprinkle with a few of the reserved basil leaves. Pile the tomato slices on top, then drizzle with more basil oil.
4 Preheat the grill until hot. Grill the tarts for 3 minutes or until the tomatoes are hot, then serve sprinkled with torn basil leaves.

Tartes aux tomates

Sweet and savoury pies, cakes and pastries are traditional English farmhouse fare. What makes these dishes particularly special is the creative use of pastry – home-made and bought – which can be cut or moulded into almost any shape. Try trimming your pies with decorations to match the contents.

pies & *pastries*

Apple and pear puffs

Makes 8

2 dessert apples
2 ripe pears
1 tbsp fresh lemon juice
115g/4oz white almond paste
450g/1lb puff pastry, thawed if frozen
beaten egg, to glaze
icing sugar, for dusting

1 Preheat the oven to 200C/400F/Gas 6. Lightly grease and dampen two baking sheets. Peel the apples and pears and brush with lemon juice. Halve, remove the cores, then slice diagonally across the tops, almost through each half. Divide the almond paste into eight and press a piece into each core cavity.
2 Roll out pastry on a lightly floured surface to 3mm/⅛ in thick. Place an apple on the pastry and trim leaving a 1cm/½ in border. Use trimmings to make a stem and leaf and secure with water.
3 Transfer to the baking sheet. Score the pastry just around the apple base. Brush with beaten egg and flute edges. Prepare remaining fruit in the same way, leaving pear pastry edges unfluted.
4 Bake for 10-15 minutes until well risen and golden. Preheat grill to high. Dust pastries generously with icing sugar, then grill for 2 minutes, watching, until glazed. These puffs are delicious served warm or cold.

Clockwise from right:
Apple and pear puffs, Orchard fruit cake,
Sweet pumpkin pie

Orchard fruit cake

Serves 12

225g/8oz self-raising flour
pinch of salt
175g/6oz lightly salted butter, diced
140g/5oz caster sugar
55g/2oz ground almonds
1 tsp almond essence
3 eggs, lightly beaten
3 tbsp milk
3 red-skinned dessert apples, cored and sliced
4 red plums, stoned and sliced
115g/4oz blackberries
25g/1oz slivered or flaked almonds
icing sugar, for dusting

1 Preheat the oven to 180C/350F/Gas 4. Grease and line the base of a 23cm/9in spring release or loose-bottomed cake tin.
2 Sift the flour and salt and blend with the butter in a food processor until the mixture starts to bind together. Or rub in butter with your fingertips until it resembles fine breadcrumbs. Beat in the sugar, ground almonds, almond essence, eggs and milk.
3 Stir in two-thirds of the apples and turn the mixture into the tin, then level the surface.
4 Mix the remaining apple slices with the plums and blackberries and scatter over the top, spreading the fruit to the edges. Sprinkle with the almonds. Bake for 1-1¼ hours or until a skewer inserted comes out clean. Remove from the tin and leave to cool. Serve dusted with icing sugar.

Sweet pumpkin pie

Serves 8

FOR THE PASTRY

280g/10oz plain flour
pinch of salt
1 tsp ground cinnamon
175g/6oz unsalted butter, diced
2 tbsp caster sugar
beaten egg and icing sugar, to glaze

FOR THE FILLING

1.8kg/4lb pumpkin, skinned, seeded and cut into chunks
300ml/½ pint double cream
1 tbsp ground mixed spice
25g/1oz fresh root ginger, grated
115g/4oz caster sugar
finely grated rind of 2 lemons

1 Make the pastry: sift the flour, salt and cinnamon in a food processor and blend with the butter until the mixture resembles fine bread-crumbs. Or rub in the butter with your fingertips. Stir in the sugar and about two tablespoons of cold water to make a firm dough. Lightly knead, then chill for 30 minutes.
2 Half-fill a large pan with water and bring to the boil. Place the pumpkin in a colander or steamer over the water. Cover with a lid or foil and steam for about 20 minutes until tender. Cool.
3 Turn two-thirds of the pumpkin into a large pie dish. Blend the remaining pumpkin with the cream, spice, ginger, sugar and lemon rind. Pour into the dish.
4 Preheat oven to 200C/400F/Gas 6. Roll out the pastry on a lightly floured surface. Dampen the rim of the dish, cover with the pastry, making a hole in the centre, then brush with egg. Use the trimmings to decorate and bake for 25 minutes or until golden.
5 Preheat the grill to high. Dust the pastry with the icing sugar and grill for 3-4 minutes until glazed. Serve warm.

Lamb and apricot pies

Makes 8

FOR THE PASTRY

450g/1lb plain flour
pinch of salt
115g/4oz butter, diced
115g/4oz white vegetable fat, diced

FOR THE FILLING

2 tbsp olive oil
350g/12oz lean minced lamb
1 small onion, chopped
2 garlic cloves, crushed
1 tbsp chopped fresh rosemary
1/4 tsp ground allspice
grated rind of 1/2 orange
1 tbsp white wine vinegar
1/2 tsp caster sugar
salt and pepper
4 ready-to-eat apricots, thinly sliced
beaten egg, to glaze

1 Make the pastry: sift the flour and salt and blend in a food processor with the butter and fat until it resembles fine breadcrumbs. Or rub in the fats with your fingertips. Add enough water to mix to a firm dough. Knead lightly and chill for 30 minutes.

2 Make the filling: heat the oil, add the lamb and fry quickly to brown. Add the onion, garlic, rosemary, allspice, orange rind, vinegar, sugar and season. Simmer for 15 minutes, then cool.

3 Preheat the oven to 190C/375F/Gas 5. Roll out the pastry and line eight individual Yorkshire pudding tins or tartlet cases. Reserve trimmings for the tops.

4 Pack the meat filling into the cases and cover with the apricot slices. Brush the edges of the pastry with beaten egg. Roll out the trimmings, cut into thin strips and use to garnish. Glaze the pastry with beaten egg and bake for 35 minutes or until golden. Leave to cool in the tins, then lift out using a palette knife.

VARIATION

Pork and cranberry pies

Make as above using minced pork instead of lamb. Substitute sage for the rosemary and 115g/4oz fresh cranberries for the apricots.

Layered chicken, pork and bacon loaf

Makes 8-10 slices

FOR THE PASTRY

450g/1lb plain flour
1/2 tsp salt
115g/4oz white vegetable fat, diced
beaten egg, to glaze

FOR THE FILLING

140g/5oz leeks, green ends
450g/1lb pork sausagemeat
1 small onion, finely chopped
2 garlic cloves, crushed
1/4 tsp freshly grated nutmeg
1 tbsp chopped fresh thyme
70g/2 1/2 oz pistachio nuts
8 rashers rindless streaky bacon
1 large skinless chicken breast, cut into strips
10 stoned ready-to-eat prunes
2 sheets leaf gelatine
300ml/1/2 pint chicken stock
salt and pepper

1 Preheat the oven to 200C/400F/Gas 6. Lay a triple thickness piece of greaseproof paper inside a 900g/2lb loaf tin, to line the base, the sides and to overhang the edges.

2 Make the pastry: sift the flour and salt into a bowl. Melt the fat with 225ml/8fl oz of water in a small pan. Bring to the boil and pour gradually over the flour, stirring constantly, to make a soft dough. Add a little more hot water if the mixture is too dry.

3 Roll out two thirds of the dough (be sure to keep the remainder covered), and use this to line the base and sides of the tin. Trim off any excess around the top. Line with greaseproof paper and lightly pack with crumpled foil, then bake blind for 15 minutes. Remove the greaseproof paper and leave to cool.

4 Blanch the leeks for 1 minute, drain. Mix the sausagemeat with the onion, garlic, nutmeg, thyme, pistachios and seasoning. Pack half the sausagemeat into the pastry case. Cover with half the leeks and half the bacon. Lay over the chicken strips and prunes and season. Cover with remaining leeks, bacon and sausagemeat. Brush top edges of the pastry with egg.

5 Roll out half the reserved pastry and cover the pie, sealing edges. Make a hole in the centre and brush with egg. Use remaining pastry for leaves and arrange around the hole. Glaze and bake for 15 minutes.

Layered chicken, pork and bacon loaf

6 Reduce oven temperature to 180C/350F/Gas 4
and bake for 1½ hours. Cover with foil if pastry
starts to over-brown. Leave in the tin for 20
minutes, lift out and cool completely.

7 Soak the leaf gelatine in two tablespoons of
water for 5 minutes. Bring the stock to the boil,
stir in the gelatine until dissolved. Leave the stock
to cool but not set, then pour into the pie through
the hole. Chill for several hours before serving.

These stunning cakes are a must for any special occasion and are well worth the time and effort they take to make. Decorated with chocolate squiggles, coils or swirls, they not only look beautiful but are also rich and delicious to eat. Either serve them at a very special tea party or as an elegant finale to lunch or dinner.

gorgeous
gateaux

Coffee and amaretti gateau

Serves 12

FOR THE SPONGE

6 eggs, separated
175g/6oz caster sugar
85g/3oz plain flour, sifted
85g/3oz ground almonds
55g/2oz amaretti biscuits, finely crushed
4 tbsp Amaretto liqueur
175g/6oz amaretti biscuits, coarsely crushed

FOR THE BUTTER CREAM

5 tsp instant coffee
5 tsp cornflour
200ml/7fl oz milk
4 tbsp caster sugar
3 egg yolks
250g/9oz butter, softened
140g/5oz icing sugar, sifted

FOR THE CHOCOLATE SHAPES AND DECORATIONS

100g/3$\frac{1}{2}$ oz plain chocolate, melted
12 mini macaroons

1 Make the sponge:
Preheat the oven to 190C/375F/Gas 5. Grease and line two 20cm/8in round sandwich tins with greased greaseproof paper. Grease the sides and dust with flour.
• Whisk yolks and 55g/2oz caster sugar with an electric whisk until pale, thick and mousse-like. Rinse the whisk and whisk the egg whites in a separate bowl until stiff, then whisk in the remaining sugar.
• Using a metal spoon, fold the egg whites, flour, almonds and the fine amaretti crumbs into the yolk mixture, taking care not to knock out the air.
• Divide the mixture between the tins and bake for 30-35 minutes or until golden. Turn out and cool on racks. (*Continued over.*)

Chocolate rose gateau (top)
and Coffee and amaretti gateau (below)

2 Make the butter cream:
Place the coffee and cornflour in a small pan, add the milk and stir continuously over a low heat until it thickens. Remove the pan from the heat, add the sugar and beat in the egg yolks. Return the pan to the heat and cook for 1 minute, stirring continuously. Leave to cool for 10 minutes, then gradually beat in the butter and icing sugar until smooth. Leave to cool until firm.

3 Assemble the gateau:
Split both cakes in half horizontally (reserve one top half for the top layer of the gateau) and drizzle the other three cakes with Amaretto. Use half the butter cream to spread over each of the three cakes. Reserve one-third of the coarsely crushed amaretti biscuits and divide remainder among the cakes. Layer up the three cakes and finish with reserved top layer. Place four tablespoons of butter cream in a piping bag with a large star nozzle and set aside for decorating. Spread the top and sides of the cake with the remaining butter cream. Smooth a cake decorator's 'comb' around the cake and sprinkle remaining amaretti biscuits around the base. Mark the top of the cake into 12 equal sections using a long knife or a ruler.

4 Make the decorations:
Melt the chocolate in a heatproof bowl over a pan of simmering water. Place half in a greaseproof paper piping bag and snip end. Pipe 'S' shapes on each marked section. Decorate the edge of each section with piped butter cream swirls. Make chocolate fans (see Tip box).

• Half dip each macaroon in the remaining melted chocolate and rest against the cream swirls. Top with chocolate fans. This cake keeps in the fridge for 4 days.

TIP

To make the chocolate fans, trace 12 fan templates on to card and place under waxed paper. Place the remaining chocolate in a greaseproof piping bag, snip the end and pipe over the traced templates. Leave to cool until set, then lift off the decorations with the point of a knife and place on the gateau.

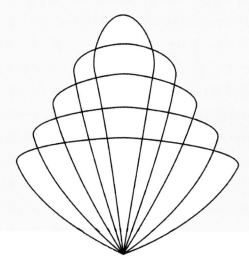

Chocolate rose gateau

Serves 8-10

For the Sponge

4 medium eggs
100g/3¹/₂ oz caster sugar
85g/3oz plain flour
25g/1oz cocoa powder
2 tbsp rum
4 tbsp apricot jam, warmed
  and sieved
1 chocolate Flake bar

For the Ganache

300ml/¹/₂ pint double cream
350g/12oz plain chocolate, chopped
40g/1¹/₂ oz butter, softened

For the Modelling Paste

100g/3¹/₂ oz luxury white cooking chocolate
2 tbsp liquid glucose

1 Make the sponge:
Preheat the oven to 190C/375F/Gas 5. Grease a 20cm/8in deep loose-bottomed cake tin and line the base with greased greaseproof paper. Dust the sides with a little flour.
• Place eggs and sugar in a bowl and set over a pan of simmering water. Using an electric whisk, beat until thick and mousse-like and the mixture leaves a trail when the whisk is lifted.
• Sift the flour and cocoa over the egg mixture, then use a large metal spoon to fold the mixture together, taking care not to knock out the air.
• Pour the mixture into the tin, bake in the centre of the oven for 35-45 minutes or until firm to the touch; turn out and cool on a wire rack.
2 Make the ganache:
Bring the cream to the boil, stir in the chocolate until melted. Pour one-third into a bowl and allow to cool. When cool, beat in the butter until smooth and shiny. Leave remaining ganache at room temperature for coating.
• Split the sponge in half horizontally. Sprinkle with some of the rum, moistening well. Spread with a little apricot jam and buttery chocolate ganache. Place remaining sponge half on top and sprinkle with more rum. Coat top and sides of cake with remaining buttery ganache. Chill in the fridge until firm.
• Place the gateau on a wire rack and pour over the thin chocolate ganache. If it is not of a pouring consistency, warm very gently. Leave to set, then decorate the base with broken pieces of chocolate Flake.
3 Make the chocolate roses:
Melt the chocolate and stir in the glucose until it leaves the sides of the bowl. Wrap in plastic film, then leave until firm. Make a small piece into a cone shape. Flatten small balls the size of peas into thin circles the size of 50p pieces. Wrap around the cone. Continue until you have a 'rose' with four to five petals. Place in fridge to firm up. Make three roses in all. To make leaves, shape paste into ovals and mark veins with the back of a knife. If you wish, make a small piece of plain chocolate modelling paste and roll into a long, thin stem. Place on the cake with roses and leaves.

Cream cheese and fruit torte

Serves 8-10

FOR THE CHOCOLATE BISCUIT PASTE

25g/1oz butter
25g/1oz icing sugar, sifted
2 tbsp beaten egg
15g/¹/₂ oz plain flour, sifted
15g/¹/₂ oz cocoa powder, sifted

FOR THE ALMOND SPONGE

100g/3¹/₂ oz ground almonds
125g/4¹/₂ oz icing sugar, sifted
25g/1oz plain flour, sifted
2 whole eggs
25g/1oz butter, melted
2 egg whites

FOR THE FRUIT FILLING

3 tbsp apricot or fruit liqueur
5 fresh apricots
3 leaves gelatine
150ml/¹/₄ pint milk
2 egg yolks
100g/3¹/₂ oz caster sugar
grated rind and juice of 1 lemon
225g/8oz full fat cream cheese
300ml/¹/₂ pint double cream
whipped double cream and fresh fruit, to decorate

1 Make the chocolate biscuit paste:
Preheat the oven to 200C/400F/Gas 6. Grease
and line a 30 x 23cm/12 x 9in Swiss roll tin with
non-stick baking paper. Cut out a 20cm/8in circle
of non-stick baking paper and place this on a
baking sheet.
• Melt the butter and stir in the remaining
ingredients until smooth. Place in a greaseproof
paper piping bag and snip off 5mm/¹/₄ in from the
end. Pipe a thin squiggly design over the circle of
non-stick baking paper to make the top
decoration, reserving some of the mixture in the
piping bag. Bake for just 3-4 minutes.

• Remove the baking sheet from the oven and
place upside-down on another sheet of non-stick
baking paper. Peel off the paper and cool. Pipe
the remaining chocolate biscuit paste on to the
Swiss roll tin in dots. Freeze for 5-10 minutes
while you are making the almond sponge.

2 Make the almond sponge:
Mix the ground almonds, 100g/3½ oz icing sugar, the flour, whole eggs and melted butter together. Whisk the egg whites in a separate bowl until they form soft peaks. Whisk in the remaining icing sugar and, using a large metal spoon, fold the egg whites into the almond mixture. Pour over the frozen chocolate dots in the tin and gently shake mixture to cover. Bake for 7-8 minutes until golden brown. Turn out on to a wire rack to cool and peel off the baking paper.

• Cut the sponge into two long strips, each about 5cm/2in deep and use to line, patterned side out, the sides of a deep 20cm/8in round loose-bottomed cake tin. Cut the remaining cake into triangles and arrange these around the base of the cake tin.

3 Make the fruit filling:
Sprinkle the sponge with the liqueur. Plunge the apricots into boiling water for 1 minute, drain and plunge into cool water. Peel off the skins and cut the fruit in half. Remove stones and arrange fruit in cake tin.

• Break up the gelatine, place in a bowl with two tablespoons of water and leave to soften for 5 minutes. Make the custard: place the milk in a pan and bring to boiling point. Mix the yolks and sugar, then pour the milk on to the mixture, stirring well. Return to the pan. Cook over a low heat until it coats the back of a spoon – do not allow to boil otherwise it will curdle. Add the drained gelatine and stir until it is dissolved.

• Stir the lemon rind and juice into the cream cheese and beat until it is really smooth. Whisk in the custard.

• Whip the cream until it forms soft peaks. Fold into the cheese mixture and pour into the cake tin. Smooth the surface and chill until it is firm. Remove the torte from the tin and carefully place chocolate biscuit pattern on top. Using a small star nozzle, pipe swirls of cream on top and decorate with fresh fruit.

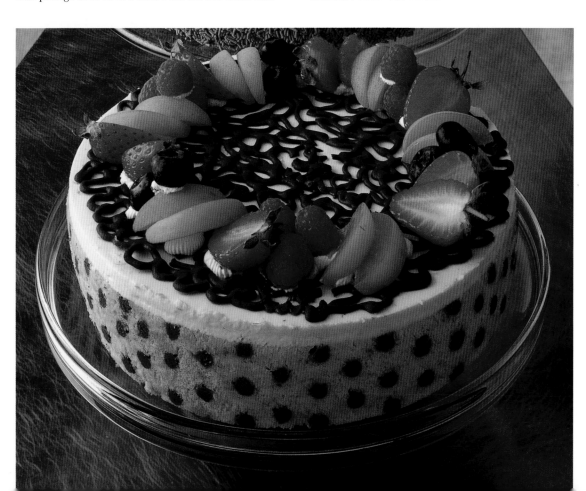

Sometimes it's difficult to know what to give family and friends for birthdays and Christmas. But you can never go wrong with edible gifts and delicious home-made dishes. Presented in beautifully wrapped jars, boxes or bags, they will be appreciated by everyone. The recipes can be made several days, if not weeks, before the event but be sure to stick an unobtrusive label on to the packaging giving the use by date and best method of storage.

gourmet *gifts*

Turkish delight (left), Assorted fudge (centre),
Chocolate candied orange peel (right)

Turkish delight

Take your pick, you can make pink, green or yellow, or best of all make a mixture.

Makes 500g/1lb 2oz

8 sheets leaf gelatine
450g/1lb granulated sugar
1/2 tsp tartaric acid
2 tbsp rosewater, crème de menthe, or fresh lemon juice
pink and yellow food colouring
50g/1 3/4 oz pistachio nuts, skinned and halved (optional)
3 tbsp icing sugar
1 tbsp cornflour

1 Wet the inside of a shallow 18cm/7in square tin with water. Soak the gelatine in four tablespoons of water in a bowl. Place the bowl in a pan of hot water and stir until dissolved.

2 Place 250ml/9fl oz of water and the sugar in a pan. Heat gently, stirring, until the sugar has dissolved. Bring to the boil and boil rapidly until it reaches 127C on a sugar thermometer.

3 For pink Turkish delight: stir the tartaric acid, rosewater and pink food colouring into the gelatine until well blended then add to the boiling syrup. For green: add the tartaric acid and crème de menthe to the gelatine and for yellow, the tartaric acid, lemon juice and yellow food colouring. Remove the syrup from the heat and add the pistachio nuts, if using. Pour into the tin and leave to set overnight.

4 Sift the icing sugar and cornflour on to a piece of greaseproof paper. Dip the base of the tin in hot water and invert on to the icing sugar. Cover each surface with the icing sugar mixture, then, using a lightly oiled knife, cut into neat squares. Toss the squares in the remainder of the icing sugar mixture to coat evenly and arrange in attractive boxes.

• Keep cool, stored in an airtight plastic container for up to 1 month

Assorted fudge

Makes 1kg/2¼ lb

50g/1¾ oz unsalted butter
450g/1lb granulated sugar
300ml/½ pint double cream
150ml/¼ pint milk
3 tbsp water, strong coffee or liqueur
1 tsp vanilla essence

FLAVOURINGS

100g/3½ oz almonds, hazelnuts, walnuts or
*   pecan nuts OR*
100g/3½ oz chopped glacé cherries, dried
*   apricots or dates*
150g/5½ oz plain or milk chocolate
icing sugar, cocoa powder, to dust
25g/1oz melted chocolate (optional)

1 Butter a shallow 20cm/8in square tin. Place the butter, sugar, cream, milk, water, coffee or liqueur and vanilla essence in a large pan. Heat very gently, stirring occasionally, until the sugar has completely dissolved.
2 Bring to the boil and reduce the heat slightly so the mixture boils steadily. Stir occasionally, to prevent the mixture burning at the bottom of the pan, until the mixture reaches 113C on a sugar thermometer, or the soft ball stage. Test by dropping a little of the mixture into a bowl of cold water. When rolled between the fingers, a soft ball is formed. Remove the pan from the heat. Add the nuts or fruit.
3 For chocolate fudge: beat in the chocolate thoroughly with a wooden spoon until it starts to thicken and become opaque, then add the nuts or fruit. Carefully pour into the tin.
4 Cool and mark into squares. When completely cold, turn out on a board and cut. Dust some with icing sugar, some with cocoa and drizzle some with melted chocolate, if using.

• Store in an airtight container for up to 6 weeks.

Chocolate candied orange peel

Makes 500g/1lb 2oz

6 large oranges
250g/9oz granulated sugar
250g/9oz plain chocolate, melted

1 Cut each orange in half and squeeze the juice (you will need 300ml/½ pint). Remove flesh and cut away some of the white pith, then slice the peel into 5mm/¼ in strips. Place in a pan and cover with water. Bring to the boil and simmer until the peel is tender, then drain.
2 Place the orange juice and sugar in a pan and heat gently, stirring occasionally, until the sugar has dissolved. Add the peel and boil for 10-15 minutes, until there is only a sticky syrup remaining.
3 Remove the peel, separating the pieces and leave to set on non-stick baking paper. When cold, dip half of each piece into the melted chocolate. Allow excess chocolate to fall back into the bowl and place on the paper to set.
4 Pack into some cellophane bags or boxes and tie with ribbon.

• Store in an airtight container for up to 1 month.

Clementines in brandy

Makes 500g/1lb 2oz

1kg/2¹/₄ lb clementines
2 bay leaves
250g/9oz granulated sugar
150ml/¹/₄ pint brandy or Cointreau

1 Using a sharp knife, cut the peel away from
the clementines including the white pith. Place
in warm, sterilized jars with the bay leaves.
2 Heat the sugar and 300ml/¹/₂ pint water in a
pan until the sugar has dissolved. Bring to the
boil. Boil rapidly until the syrup reaches 110C
on a sugar thermometer, or the thread stage.
Test by pressing a small amount of syrup
between two teaspoons. When the spoons are
pulled apart, a thread should form between
them. Leave to cool.
3 Measure the syrup and add the same amount
of brandy and stir. Pour over the fruit so that it
is completely covered.

• Seal jars with airtight lids and keep for up to
1 month.

Marinated goat's cheese

Makes 2 x 250g/9oz jars

300ml/¹/₂ pint olive oil
2 x 100g/3¹/₂ oz full fat soft goat's cheese
2 tsp mixed peppercorns
2 sun-dried tomatoes, cut into small pieces
1 tsp mixed dried herbs
1 tsp sea salt

1 Half-fill two 250g/9oz sterilized jars with oil.
Thinly slice the cheese and place in the jars
with the peppercorns, tomato pieces, herbs and
the salt. Fill the jars to the top with the
remaining oil and cover. Store in a cool place.

• Store for up to 1 month in the fridge.

Scottish black bun

This traditional fruit bun is made in Scotland for Hogmanay. Instead of baking it in its usual pastry wrapping, we have used marzipan.

Makes 2 fruit buns

100g/3¹/₂ oz melted butter
500g/1lb 2oz luxury mixed dried fruit
50g/1³/₄ oz blanched almonds, chopped
50g/1³/₄ oz dried apricots, chopped
2 tsp grated orange rind
2 tbsp whisky
100g/3¹/₂ oz dark muscovado sugar
2 eggs, beaten
100g/3¹/₂ oz plain flour
1 tsp ground allspice
2 tbsp apricot jam, boiled and sieved
500g/1lb 2oz white marzipan
green and purple food colourings

1 Preheat the oven to 150C/300F/Gas 2. Cut out two 25cm/10in squares of greaseproof paper and two squares of foil. Place the greaseproof squares on top of the foil squares and brush lightly with melted butter.

2 Mix together the mixed fruit, almonds, apricots, orange rind, and whisky. Stir in the sugar, remaining butter and eggs. Sift in the flour and allspice and beat until blended.

3 Divide the mixture between the paper squares, draw up the edges of the paper to the centre and twist into a neat round. Repeat with the foil. Place on a baking sheet and bake for 1¹/₄ hours or until the mixture feels firm when pressed.

4 Remove the foil covering and return the rounds in paper to the oven for 20-30 minutes. Cool on a wire rack.

5 Preheat the grill to hot. Remove the paper and brush the cakes with apricot jam. Cut off a quarter of the marzipan and reserve. Cut remainder in half and roll out one half into a round large enough to cover one cake. Tuck edges under and mould into a smooth round. Make sure the cake is completely enclosed in the marzipan so that it keeps. Repeat for the second cake. Place the cakes on a foil-lined tray and place under the grill until the marzipan is evenly browned. Leave until cold.

6 Colour half the remaining marzipan green and half purple. Cut out two purple thistle shapes and two green thistle stems and leaves using small holly-shaped pastry cutters. Mark in the details with a knife and arrange on the cake.

• These cakes can be stored in a cake tin for up to 1 month.

Scottish black bun

Pâté

Makes 6 small, 4 medium or 1 large terrine

200g/7oz chicken livers
200g/7oz skinless duck breasts, sliced
1 onion, roughly chopped
1 garlic clove
2 tbsp roughly chopped fresh sage
100g/3¹/₂ oz fresh white breadcrumbs
1 egg
1 tbsp Marsala
150ml/¹/₄ pint chicken stock
1 sheet leaf gelatine
salt and freshly ground black pepper
fresh cranberries and bay leaves, to garnish

1 Preheat oven to 160C/325F/Gas 3. Place the chicken livers, duck breasts, onion, garlic, seasoning and sage in a food processor. Process until smooth.
2 Add the breadcrumbs, egg and Marsala and process until smooth. Spoon the mixture into dishes and cover with a layer of greaseproof paper and foil. Seal well.
3 Stand the dishes in a roasting tin with hot water to come halfway up the sides of the dishes. Bake for 45 minutes – 1 hour or until firm to the touch. Remove the dishes from the tin, release the foil and allow the steam to escape. Seal well, place a weight on top of each dish to flatten and leave the pâté until cold.
4 Soak the gelatine in a little stock, add to the pan with the remaining stock and heat until the gelatine has dissolved. Cool, then arrange the cranberries and bay leaves on the pâté. When the stock is cold, spoon over the top of each dish and chill until it is set. Cover with plastic film and keep chilled.

• Store in the fridge for up to 2-3 days, or freeze for up to 1 month.

Pudding should be the crowning glory of a special meal and for your peace of mind, it helps to have it prepared in advance so there is no panic just before serving. All these desserts can be made at least one day before the meal and require very little, if any, last-minute work.

For example, the almond meringue for the Pavlova can happily be made a week in advance and assembled up to one hour before the meal, while the Iced pudding can be made one month ahead.

perfect puddings

Chocolate mille feuille

This pudding can be made, assembled and frozen, in a rigid container, weeks before it is needed. Transfer on to a serving plate and place in the fridge for 1-2 hours before serving, decorated with the fruit and nuts.

Serves 8

175g/6oz plain chocolate, broken into pieces
250g/9oz mascarpone cheese
1 tbsp caster sugar
4 tbsp Amaretto liqueur or brandy
300ml/^{1}/$_2$ pint double cream
85g/3oz toasted blanched almonds, chopped
140g/5oz milk chocolate, grated

To Decorate

white chocolate curls, shaved from a block of
  chocolate using a sharp knife
115g/4oz Cape gooseberries
15g/^{1}/$_2$ oz toasted almonds, roughly chopped

1 Melt the chocolate in a heatproof bowl over a pan of simmering water. Cut out four 27 x 15cm/10^3/$_4$ x 6in foil rectangles. Spread the chocolate over the foil to within 2cm/ ^{3}/$_4$ in of the edges. Place several pencils on baking sheets, then position the foil rectangles on top, so that the chocolate sets in a corrugated pattern. Chill or leave in a cool place to set.
2 Beat the mascarpone with the sugar, then beat in the liqueur and cream until softly peaking. Fold in the almonds and the milk chocolate.
3 Carefully peel the foil away from the chocolate layers. Place one layer on a plate or lid of a freezer container. Spread with a third of the cream mixture, then add a second chocolate layer. Repeat layering, finishing with a chocolate layer. Scatter generously with chocolate curls. Cover and freeze.
4 Transfer to a flat serving plate and place in the fridge for 1-2 hours, then decorate with the Cape gooseberries and almonds.

Plum and caramelized almond Pavlova

Pavlova makes an eye-catching dessert for a dinner party or family get-together. The almond meringue can be made up to a week in advance and kept in an airtight container. Don't be tempted to assemble too far in advance of eating; once the meringue is in touch with the filling it will slowly start to soften and go very soggy.

Serves 8

FOR THE MERINGUE

85g/3oz flaked almonds
1 tbsp icing sugar, sifted
4 egg whites
225g/8oz caster sugar
1 tsp cornflour
1 tsp almond essence

FOR THE FILLING

700g/1lb 9oz dessert plums, stoned and quartered
2 tbsp caster sugar
200ml (20cl) tub crème fraîche
300ml/¹/2 pint vanilla yogurt
fresh plum or damson leaves, to decorate

1 Preheat the grill to hot. Spread the flaked almonds over a baking sheet, dust with half the icing sugar, then briefly cook under the grill until caramelized and golden. Shake the sheet to turn the almonds over, dust with the remaining icing sugar, then grill again until golden. Watch the almonds all the time as they caramelize very quickly. Cool, finely chop two-thirds and set aside.
2 Preheat the oven to 140C/275F/Gas 1. Line a large baking sheet with non-stick baking paper and draw a 20cm/8in circle in the centre.
3 Make the meringue: whisk the egg whites until they form soft peaks, then gradually whisk in the caster sugar and cornflour, whisking well, until you have a stiff, glossy meringue.
4 Fold in the chopped almonds and almond essence, then spread the meringue within the circle, right to the edges and slightly hollow the centre to make a nest shape.

5 Scatter with half the remaining almonds, then bake for 1-1¼ hours until pale golden and crisp. Turn off the oven and leave the meringue inside for 1 hour before removing.
6 Make the filling: cook the plums and sugar in a pan until the juices start to run, then leave to cool.
7 Just before serving, whip the crème fraîche until softly peaking, fold in the yogurt, then spoon into the centre of the meringue. Arrange plums on top, scatter over almonds and decorate with the leaves.

Coconut and meringue ice

Unlike many home-made ice cream recipes, this doesn't contain raw eggs, or need to be beaten once it goes into the freezer where it will keep for three months.

Serves 4

450g/1lb plums
225g/8oz granulated sugar
200ml carton coconut cream
300ml/¹/2 pint whipping cream, lightly whipped
2 ready-made meringue nests (about 25g/1oz),
*   coarsely crushed*
plum leaves, to decorate
ice cream biscuits, to serve

1 Place the plums, sugar and three tablespoons of water in a pan, stir over a gentle heat until the sugar dissolves, then cover and simmer for 20 minutes until the plums are tender. Remove and discard stones and cool.
2 Stir the coconut cream into the plums, then carefully fold in the cream and meringue.
3 Pour the mixture into a rigid container, then freeze on the fast freeze setting for at least 4 or so hours.
4 Serve straight from the freezer in scoops, decorated with some plum leaves and with ice cream biscuits.

Plum and caramelized almond Pavlova (top),
and Coconut and meringue ice (below)

Christmas crackers

These pastry crackers may be served warm or cold. Shape, freeze uncooked and place in a rigid container. Interleave the crackers with layers of greaseproof paper.

Makes 12-14

1 cooked apple, peeled and grated
115g/4oz cranberries, thawed if frozen
225g/8oz mincemeat
1/4 tsp ground mixed spice
2 tbsp Cointreau or orange flavoured liqueur
200g/7oz filo pastry
40g/1 1/2 oz unsalted butter, melted
icing sugar, for dusting

1 Preheat the oven to 200C/400F/Gas 6. Lightly grease a large baking sheet. Place the apple in a pan with the cranberries and cook until the fruits are soft and the juices have evaporated. Stir in the mincemeat, spice and liqueur and leave to cool.
2 Lay one sheet of filo pastry on a clean work surface. Keep the remainder covered with a damp tea towel, or plastic film to prevent them from drying out. Lightly brush the filo with butter and cover with a second sheet. Brush with more butter. Cut out 13cm/5in squares. (Filo sheets vary in size, depending on the brand. You may need to adjust the size of the squares to avoid wastage.)
3 Place a heaped dessertspoon of cranberry mixture into the centre of one square and roll up the pastry around it. Pinch the pastry firmly together, about 2cm/3/4in from the ends, to create a cracker shape. Transfer to the baking sheet and make the remaining crackers in the same way.
4 Brush crackers with more butter and bake for 15-20 minutes or until golden. Serve warm or cold, lightly dusted with icing sugar.

Iced pudding

Once frozen, this pudding may be stored for up to 1 month. Turn out on to a serving plate and place in the fridge for 30 minutes to soften before serving. Pour over the sauce after turning out, or just before serving.

Serves 12

85g/3oz sultanas
85g/3oz raisins
55g/2oz candied orange peel, finely chopped
125ml/4fl oz brandy
600ml/1 pint whipping cream
140g/5oz caster sugar
1/4 tsp ground cinnamon
1/4 tsp ground nutmeg
grated rind of 1 lemon and 1 orange
55g/2oz broken walnuts

TO DECORATE

115g/4oz plain chocolate, broken into pieces
1 tbsp brandy

1 Place the sultanas, raisins and candied orange peel in a bowl. Add the brandy and leave for several hours or overnight until the fruits have mostly absorbed the brandy.
2 Whip the cream until beginning to thicken. Add the sugar and spices and whip until very softly peaking. Stir in the lemon and orange rind, walnuts and brandy-soaked fruits. Turn into a 1.2 litre/2 pint pudding basin and freeze for at least 8 hours until firm.
3 To turn out, dip the basin into very hot water for 2 seconds, then loosen the pudding by twisting a fork in the centre. Invert on to a serving plate and either return to the freezer or place in the fridge for 30 minutes.
4 Melt the chocolate and the brandy in a heat-proof bowl over a pan of simmering water. Allow to cool slightly if quite hot, then spoon or pour over the pudding.

Iced pudding

home
work

I think it's only ever worth taking the trouble to make things yourself if they're going to be cheaper, better or different than buying them ready-made. All these ideas for the home are easy and effective, and I can guarantee you'll have fun doing them, too. Whether you keep them for yourself or give them to family and friends as presents, they'll give great pleasure for many years, and you'll get enormous satisfaction from knowing that you can't buy them in the shops.

Personalized gifts, to celebrate special occasions, are great fun to make and are always treasured by whoever receives them. If like most of us you don't feel particularly artistic, découpage – the art of creating a design from cut-out paper pictures – is a winner.

These decorated plates look as good as designer china but are, in fact, incredibly easy to make, and best of all, they cost next to nothing. All you need are appropriate pictures – wrapping paper and greetings cards are good sources – a sharp pair of scissors, glue, a glass plate and paint. The shiny glass surface gives the plates a professional finish and while they are not for everyday use, they are perfect for displaying on a wall.

découpage
plates

Many occasions, birthdays, weddings, anniversaries, moving house or having special new arrivals, lend themselves to mementoes. If you can incorporate photographs and make a feature of the special date, the plates are all the more impressive. Hand-writing a message or adding a poem is another way of personalizing the design. Once the plate is finished, fix a peel-and-stick hanger to the back and wrap in layers of tissue. I made one for my daughter's recent birthday and she loved it.

YOU WILL NEED

small sharp-pointed scissors • **gift wrap and/or greeting cards with appropriate motifs** • 1 clean glass plate – this one is 26cm across • **Blu-tac** • extra-fine pointed gold or black spirit-based marker pen • **striped gift wrap for the border** • PVA adhesive and paint brush • **cotton wool buds** • small sponge • **acrylic or emulsion paint** • clear varnish and paint brush

1 Selecting the motifs

Carefully cut out a selection of paper motifs and arrange on the plate to create your design. It helps to have a large motif in the centre and it is also a good idea to overlap some of the motifs. Use the Blu-tac to hold them in place.

2 Personalizing the plate

Using the marker pen, write a greeting or the baby's name and date of birth on a cut-out star or other appropriate motif. Remove the Blu-tac and the motifs from the front of the plate.

3 Sticking the design in place Starting with the main central motif, paste the right side of each motif with the PVA adhesive and stick it into place, on the back of the plate, to build up the design. It is important to remove air bubbles by rubbing your thumb nail over the back of each motif.

4 Adding the border This is made from torn strips of striped gift wrap. Snip into the paper strips at 3cm intervals to help fit around the rim of the plate, then paste into place with the torn edge towards the centre. Trim edges around rim. You can vary the width of the border to create a more interesting effect.

5 Painting the background When the design is complete and dry, clean off excess adhesive with warm water and a cotton wool bud. Dry thoroughly, then sponge paint over the back of the plate to colour the clear glass and neaten up the back of the motifs. Apply several thin coats, allowing the paint to dry in between each coat.

HINTS & TIPS

• It is best to choose glass plates that have a large flat area in the centre

• Don't worry about using plenty of the white PVA adhesive; it dries clear and any excess can easily be cleaned off with a cotton wool bud or with a damp cloth

• Small, sharp-pointed scissors make cutting out the motifs really easy

• The most successful designs are often made up from motifs cut from one sheet of wrapping paper

• Co-ordinating the colour of the motifs, border paper and the painted background is essential for a successful design

• For best results use neat acrylic paint for the background

• To write a message, as on the plates pictured on pages 42 and 43, use a gold pen and a sheet of cream paper. Write your message repeatedly then, when it is dry, tear out a centre section in a shape appropriate for the plate design.

6 Finishing touches Protect the back of the plate with a coat of clear varnish, then carefully clean up the glass surface of the plate with a sponge and warm water and rub dry until it shines. Do not submerge the plate in water.

Anything decorated with mosaic makes an up-to-date accessory for your home and many items can be covered using the basic technique shown for this table top.

Junk shops are a great source of cheap objects with a good shape, that would look better covered in colourful bits and pieces. For ease and economy, we chose to cover this table top with broken plates. It's a great project for a beginner because the table surface is flat and the design is ready-made – the plates are smashed, then pieced back together to create a simple, but effective design. The background is filled in with plain coloured broken tiles. However, once you are more practised, you can experiment with a variety of materials such as glass, shells and buttons as well as broken tiles and china. Just mix and match for your own original design. If you are a novice, it is best to start with a fairly simple item with a relatively smooth surface, such as a mirror frame, vase or a table top.

mosaic
table top

As with most projects, the key to success is in the preparation. Plan your design, mark it out on the base object and experiment with your mosaic materials until you have collected together exactly what you will need. Design, colour and texture are all important to achieve a successful finish. We found it easiest to work the mosaic using a clear adhesive, so that we could see and follow the drawn design on the surface below.

YOU WILL NEED

6 patterned earthenware tea plates • **round flat table top or 9mm plywood cut to size to match a table base – this one is 50cm across** • Blu-tac • **pencil** • small can impact adhesive • **small paint brush** • sticky-backed plastic or adhesive tape (transparent is best) • **corrugated cardboard** • hammer • **tile cutter** • 6 x 5.5mm thick dark blue tiles • **2 pairs of pliers** • rubber gloves • **medium-size packet of tile grout** • black poster paint • **large piece of sponge**

1 **Planning the design** Position the plates on the table top, several centimetres from the edge, wrong side up and in an overlapping design. Secure with Blu-tac, then draw around each one. Seal the table surface with a coat of adhesive and leave to dry for 1 hour.

2 **Breaking the plates** Cover the front of each plate with some sticky-backed plastic or adhesive tape. One at a time, sandwich each plate between corrugated cardboard, then, using the hammer, smash each plate into small pieces – at least 30.

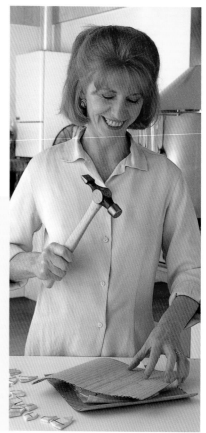

HINTS & TIPS

• Break the ridged areas of the plates into small pieces to ensure a smooth, flat surface

• To get a good smooth surface, make sure the plates and tiles are of similar thickness

• You can use tile adhesive if you already have it, but the impact adhesive is transparent, allowing you to follow the guidelines of your drawn design

• When breaking the plates, check the effect of each hammer blow before making another.

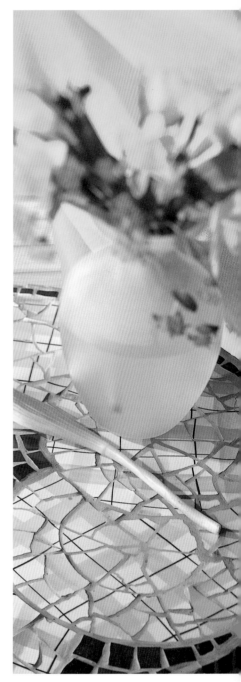

3 Creating the mosaic design

Spread the adhesive generously over one plate area of the design, going beyond the outline by about 1cm and omitting overlapping section. Peel off pieces from one broken plate and reassemble on the glued area, maintaining the pattern but leaving small gaps between the pieces for the grout. Continue building up the design with the remaining plates.

4 Adding the background

Using the tile cutter, score and snap the dark blue tiles into pieces roughly 15mm square. Spread some adhesive on to the remaining background areas and cover with the broken tile pieces. Where necessary, cut the pieces of tile even smaller by first scoring with the tile cutter, then snapping into two using the two pairs of pliers.

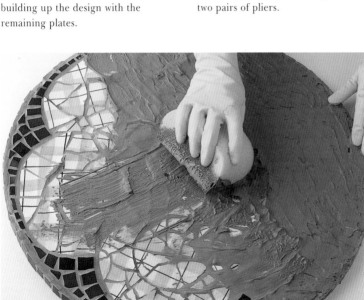

5 Neatening the table edge

Apply the adhesive to both the table edge and enough tile pieces to cover it. Leave for 15 minutes until the adhesive becomes tacky, then position the pieces. Leave the mosaic design overnight to dry thoroughly.

6 Grouting the mosaic

Wearing rubber gloves, mix up the grout following the packet instructions and add poster paint to colour. Using the sponge and starting from the centre, work the grout into the cracks until it is level with the mosaic surface. Remove excess grout with a clean damp sponge. Next day polish off the remaining film of dried grout with a soft cloth or a brush.

There is something very comforting and satisfying about working a design with a needle and thread, but I find I often start projects like this and never quite finish them. With this in mind we have designed this delightful cushion cover using really thick wool and large-hole canvas, so that the design grows wonderfully quickly.

The design, a bright tartan mixed with country cottage roses, will look good in both traditional and modern homes throughout the year. Worked in half cross stitch, the easiest of all the embroidery stitches, the finished size of the cover is 35cm square. Once completed you could think about making others to match, perhaps working just the tartan background on one cover and the roses on a plain background on another.

canvas
embroidery
cushion

Alternatively, you could make a rug repeating the design over the canvas. They would all look sensational.

Materials for making this embroidered cushion cover are available from craft shops or in a kit by mail order. For details see over.

YOU WILL NEED

46cm square of FSK/Anchor 5 mesh canvas • **masking tape** • 6 ply pure new whipping rug wool – 1 ball each of Dark Rose 13, Mid Pink 51, Pale Pink 72, Light Green 7, Dark Green 39, Yellow/Green 17, Blue 23, Navy 37, Orange 41 • **No 13 embroidery needle** • embroidery frame (optional)

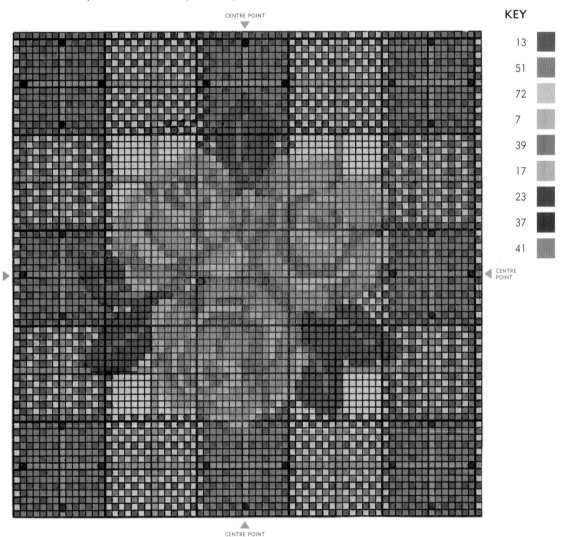

CENTRE POINT

CENTRE POINT

CENTRE POINT

CENTRE POINT

KEY

13	
51	
72	
7	
39	
17	
23	
37	
41	

This pretty design is worked on large mesh canvas – five holes to 2.5cm – in thick rug wool. It is quick to make, but is firmer with a bolder pattern than traditional tapestry. Use a heavyweight fabric for the back of the cushion.

Preparing the canvas

1 Fold the canvas in half lengthways and widthways and mark the folds. This will give you the centre of the canvas to correspond with the centre of the chart.

2 Cover the raw edges of the canvas with masking tape to prevent it from fraying and from catching on the yarn as you stitch.

3 Before starting the design, identify the wool colours with the shades in the Key above. Attach a small piece of each shade to the appropriate colour on the key for easy reference.

4 Although it is not essential, you may find it convenient to use an embroidery frame – in which case attach your canvas to the frame.

Stitching the canvas

1 The design is worked in half cross stitch throughout – start in the centre of the design and work outwards. Each square on the chart represents one half cross stitch worked on the canvas. Make sure that all your stitches slope in the same direction.

2 It is advisable to thread your needle with no more than a 50cm length of wool in the required colour. Avoid using knots to start a new piece of wool. You can work the first few stitches over the tail-end of the wool to secure it.

Straightening the canvas

1 When your design is complete, it may need to be 'blocked' in order to return the canvas to its original shape and condition. Cover a clean soft board with a piece of blotting paper on which you have drawn the correct outline of your tapestry – 46cm square. Gently moisten the back of the canvas with a fine spray of water.

2 Place the work face down on the board and pin it into shape at 2.5cm intervals using rust-free tacks or drawing pins. Keep adjusting the pins until you are satisfied that you have achieved the correct shape, then leave it to dry at room temperature. Repeat this process if necessary for a severely warped canvas.

TO MAKE UP THE CUSHION YOU WILL NEED

the worked canvas · **40cm square matching coloured furnishing fabric** · matching thread · **35cm cushion pad** · 30cm zip (optional) · **1.5m length matching coloured cord (optional)**

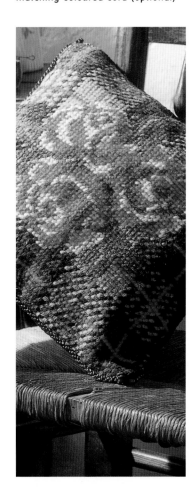

1 Trim the worked canvas, leaving a 2.5cm unworked seam allowance all the way round.

2 Place the canvas and fabric square right sides together, then pin and stitch round three sides of the cushion cover as close to the worked design as possible.

3 Trim the seams and clip the corners. Fold the canvas seam allowance back on to the worked canvas and hem in place to prevent it being felt through the fabric backing.

4 Turn the cushion through to the right side and sew a zip into the opening, if using. Alternatively, for a quick finish, simply place the cushion pad inside the cover and over-sew the opening closed.

5 If you would like to add a finishing touch, sew the matching coloured cord round the edge.

Tartan Roses kit

A kit is available to readers of *The Best of Good Living with Jane Asher*. It contains everything you need to complete the Tartan Roses design including the canvas, pure new whipping rug wool in the necessary shades, needle, chart and full instructions, price £17.99 inc p&p. The offer is available to residents of the UK and BFPO stations only while stocks last. Send your cheque or postal order, payable to Readicut Wool, together with your name and address, to Tartan Roses Offer, Dept PR600, Readicut Wool, Terry Mills, Osset, West Yorkshire WF5 9SA. Credit and Switch card holders can telephone their order through on 01924 810810. Allow at least 28 days for delivery.

How to half cross stitch

The diagram shows the needle entering into and emerging from the canvas at the same time. If you use a frame you can make the stitches using two movements and both hands. This speeds up your work and improves the regularity of the stitches. The diagram shows the direction in which to stitch. The needle comes up at A, down at B, up at C and so on.

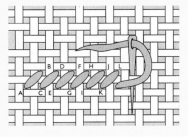

Capture the magic of the countryside in autumn with this lovely embroidered picture. After the straw colours of summer hay-making and the close of September, fruits swell and ripen into the rich colours of amber, purple and smouldering red. In this picture, designed for us by Betty Barnden, we capture rosehips, hawthorn and hazelnuts, acorns, blackberries and sloes all neatly bordered with their names and framed with fallen leaves.

While this is not a difficult picture to embroider, it will take time and skill to count the canvas threads and work the design, mostly in cross stitch and outlined in back stitch. Each square on the chart represents one cross stitch on the canvas. All the materials required to make this picture are available from craft shops or in a kit by mail order. For details see over.

cross stitch
picture

Once the embroidery is complete, it is ready to be framed. We chose a natural wooden frame to complement the embroidery, and a double card mount in light blue and grey to enhance the white of the canvas.

YOU WILL NEED

FSK/Anchor 14-count Fiddlers Aida fabric measuring 38 x 33cm for a finished size of 28 x 23cm • **11 skeins coloured Madeira cotton thread (see Key, opposite page)** • No 24 embroidery needle • **embroidery frame (optional)** • wooden frame and double card mount (optional)

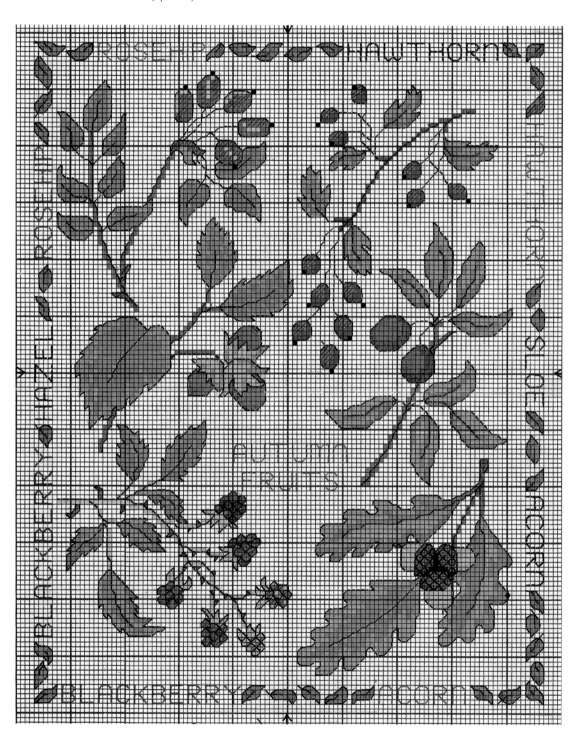

Preparing the fabric

1 Fold the fabric in half lengthways and widthways and mark the folds. This will give you the centre of the canvas to correspond with the centre of the chart.

2 Over-sew the raw edges of the fabric to prevent it from fraying and catching the yarn as you stitch.

3 Identify each colour with the shades in the Key, below. For easy reference, tape a small piece of each colour to the chart key. Madeira thread is six strands, use two strands of thread for the cross stitches and three quarter stitches. Cut the thread into 50cm lengths, separate all six strands, then recombine two strands.

4 Although it is not essential, you may find it convenient to use an embroidery frame – in which case attach your canvas to the frame.

Stitching the fabric

1 The design is worked mostly in cross stitch – start in the centre of the design and work outwards. Each square on the chart represents one cross stitch worked on the fabric, half a square represents a three quarter stitch. Make sure that all your top stitches slope in the same direction. Avoid using knots to start a new piece of thread. You can work the first few stitches over the tail-end of the thread to secure it. Finish off by threading the end beneath the last worked stitches on the wrong side. When the cross stitch design is complete, outline in back stitch following the chart and key.

CROSS STITCH

Complete each cross as you go along. Or work the first row from left to right, then complete the crosses from right to left, as above.

THREE QUARTER STITCH

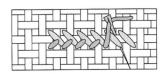

Where one square has two colour symbols, work three quarters of the stitch in one colour and the remaining one quarter in the other colour.

BACK STITCH

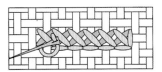

Use one strand of embroidery thread to work black back stitching and two strands to work the dark blue, purple, dark red and brown.

Straightening the embroidery

1 When your design is complete, it may need to be 'blocked' in order to return the fabric to its original shape and condition. Cover a clean soft board with a piece of blotting paper on which you have drawn the correct outline of your embroidery – 38 x 33cm. Gently moisten the back of the fabric with a fine spray of water.

2 Place the work face down on the board and pin it into shape at 2.5cm intervals using rust-free tacks or drawing pins. Keep adjusting the pins until you are satisfied that you have achieved the correct shape, then leave it to dry at room temperature. Your picture is now ready to mount and frame.

Autumn fruits kit

A kit is available to readers of *The Best of Good Living with Jane Asher*. It contains everything you need to complete the autumn fruits picture, including the fabric, Madeira threads in the necessary shades, needle, chart and full instructions, price £10.99 inc p&p (picture frame not included). The offer is available to residents of the UK and BFPO stations only while stocks last. Send your cheque or postal order, payable to Readicut Wool, together with your name and address, to Autum Fruits Offer, Dept PR599, Readicut Wool, Terry Mills, Osset, West Yorkshire WF5 9SA. Credit and Switch card holders can telephone their order through on 01924 810810. Allow 28 days for delivery.

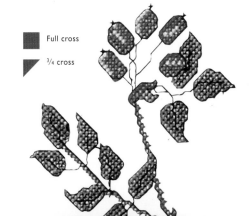

Key

Use one skein of each of the following:

Cross stitch (2 strands)		
■	Black	
▨	Dark blue	1007
▨	Purple	0714
▨	Dark red	0513
▨	Rosy red	0507
▨	Brown	2214
▨	Pale gold	2208
▨	Pale green	1414
▨	Mid green	1502
▨	Dark green	1312
▨	Grey brown	1905

Back stitch	
╲	Black (1 strand)
╱	1007 (2 strands)
╱	0714 (2 strands)
╲	0513 (2 strands)
╱	2214 (2 strands)

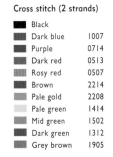

■ Full cross

◤ ³/₄ cross

Furniture is always expensive and quite often rather boring, so it's good to find something that is fun to look at and relatively cheap to make. Cover up a plain shelf unit and hide family clutter with this colourful tented cupboard.

We bought this shelving unit from a DIY store for less than £30. The basic cover uses five metres of fabric and we bought a metre each of the plain colours for bindings and the flag trims. This particular cover, using broad striped fabric, captures the essence of a seaside bathing hut making it perfect for a bathroom. With a little imagination it could be adapted to look like Dr Who's Tardis, a doll's house or even a fairy-tale castle – all of which should encourage the untidiest of children to clear away the clutter in their bedrooms.

covered *shelving*

Our unit was bought as a flat pack and needed to be assembled. The only other piece of carpentry required to make this tented cover is to screw-fix a short piece of dowelling to the centre of the top shelf. Once covered in fabric, this gives the roof its pointed tent shape. A similar fabric cover with a flat roof can be made missing out this stage. One good tip, when choosing your fabric make sure that it is opaque and machine washable.

The assembled shelf unit with roof tent pole

Annora Spenc

YOU WILL NEED

inexpensive shelving unit (this pine unit is 175cm high x 83cm wide x 30cm deep) • **screw and screwdriver** • 20cm length of 3cm dowel to create roof point • **5m x 142cm wide striped furnishing fabric** • 1m each of two plain furnishing fabrics • **matching sewing threads**

1 Making the framework If necessary, assemble the shelf unit. Screw the length of dowel to the centre of the top shelf. If you wish to add the roof flag later, drill a hole into the end of the dowel to accommodate the flag pole.

2 Measuring up the unit Following the diagram, measure the height (A), width (B), depth (C), centre front to top of dowel (D) and centre side to top of dowel (E).

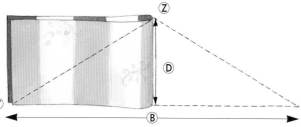

3 Cutting out roof panels For front and back panels, cut two fabric rectangles B x D, adding a 2cm seam allowance all round. Fold panels in half and cut from Y to Z (see diagram above). Repeat for two side panels, using measurements C x E. Machine stitch the four roof panels together with right sides facing.

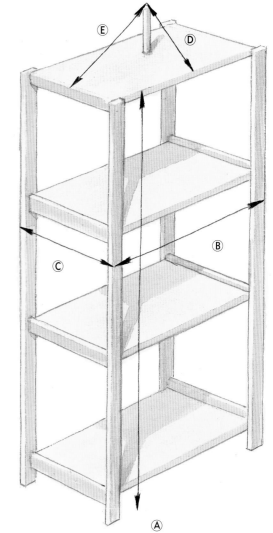

4 Making the side panels Find the circumference of the unit by adding measurements B+C+B+C + 10cm for fabric overlap. Measure the height A + 10cm for seam allowance and hem. Cut a piece of fabric to this size, joining two widths, if necessary. Also cut two turquoise fabric strips 7cm wide by the height of the fabric sides. Sew on these strips to bind the front edges of the tent sides, enclosing all raw edges.

5 Making the flagged pelmet For ease, the flags are made individually, then spaced evenly around the tent. For the pattern, cut a rectangle 17 x 25cm for the orange flags and 17 x 20cm for the shorter turquoise flags. Fold each rectangle in half and cut from corner to corner as before. Cut out 14 pairs each of orange and turquoise flags. Machine stitch each pair together along two long edges, right sides together and taking a 1cm seam allowance. Turn right side out and press.

6 Attaching the flag pelmet

Starting at the centre front, pin orange flags around the roof, matching raw edges. Repeat with turquoise flags, centring them between the orange ones. Machine stitch flags to roof.

7 Adding the tent walls

With right sides together and matching the centre back of the tent roof and tent wall panel, work around roof panels pinning the two together, finishing at the centre front with an overlap of 10cm. Machine stitch in place. Turn right side out and press.

8 Finishing touches

Place cover over unit and hem lower edge. For fun, make up an extra flag and stitch to a thin piece of dowel. Make a small hole in the centre of the roof seam and slot the flag pole through into the roof dowel below.

HINTS & TIPS

• A simpler cover can be made with a single-panelled flat roof.

• Make tiebacks to hold the cover open when in use.

• Use firm furnishing fabric for the cover. Finer fabric can be stiffened in the roof area with iron-on interfacing.

• Any old cupboard or wardrobe can be covered in a similar way, but remove the door.

• Fabric quantities depend on the size of the unit – key measurements are unit circumference and fabric width.

Suddenly, boring old shoe bags have become fashionable again. Made in all shapes and sizes and in almost any fabric, they have endless uses for holding anything from duvets to pot pourri.

A basic drawstring bag is made very easily (see next page). However, by changing the position of the casing, using different fabrics and decorating the bags in imaginative ways they take on quite a different look. Here we show you how to make lacy gift bags, colour-coded shoe bags, monogrammed school bags and a jumbo bag, large enough to hold the week's washing.

drawstring *bags*

The jumbo laundry and duvet bag

If you long for a practical way of storing duvets and sleeping bags, this is it. At 65 x 100cm, it also makes a great laundry bag.

YOU WILL NEED

120 x 136cm wide striped furnishing fabric, cut in two, vertically • 68 x 30cm wide paper strip • 150cm cord • matching sewing thread

1 Making the flagged top edging The size of the flags can match the width of your fabric stripes, or you can make a pattern. For the pattern, cut a 30cm wide paper strip by the width of the fabric pieces (68cm). Fold into three so it almost forms a square, measure up 5cm from the lower edge, then draw an inverted V-shaped flag on top and cut out the triangle. Cut a 30cm wide strip from across the width of the two fabric pieces. To create contrasting coloured flags picture, turn facings through 180º then pin, right sides together, across the top of each fabric piece. Pin the paper pattern over one fabric strip, points flush with the top edge, and draw around it. Stitch along this line, then trim off excess fabric. Turn flagging right sides out and press. Repeat for other piece.

2 Making the drawstring channel Turn under 1cm along the lower edge of each flagged facing, and machine stitch to the bag side. Make a parallel line of machine stitching 4cm above this to create the drawstring channel.

3 Making up the bag With right sides together, stitch the sides and base edges, taking a 2cm seam allowance. Leave an opening in the side seams at the channel, to create the drawstring opening. Neaten all raw edges, trim and press. Turn right side out. Thread the cord through the channel and secure the ends.

Boys' and girls' school bags

YOU WILL NEED

40 x 112cm wide pieces pink and blue gingham, cut into pieces 40cm wide · **160 x 2.5cm wide pink bias binding** · 90cm white cord · **crafters' duplicating paper or tracing paper** · 1 pink, 1 blue and 3 white 21cm felt squares · **pink embroidery thread** · 20cm square small-check pink gingham, neatened around edge with 1cm hem · **matching sewing threads** · 170cm blue cord, cut into two equal lengths

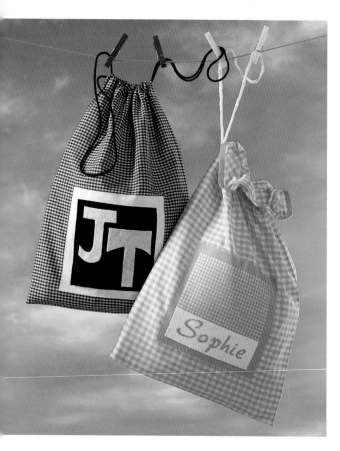

1 Making the blue bag Start by making a top drawstring channel by folding over the top edge 1cm, then 5cm to the wrong side. Machine stitch in place and again around the top folded edge. Follow the instructions for making the basic bag (see below) finishing the side seams just below the casings. Neaten, and thread the cord.

2 Decorating the blue bag This is done in a similar way to the pink bag, but uses large felt initials copied from a newspaper and enlarged on a photocopier machine. These are then cut out in white felt and stitched in place.

1 Making the pink bag Follow the instructions for making the basic bag (see below), but neaten the top edge with half the pink bias binding and make the drawstring channel 8cm down from the top edge.

2 Decorating the pink bag Write your child's name on a piece of paper, or print it from a computer. Using crafters' duplicating paper or tracing paper, transfer the lettering on to the white felt, then stitch the letters by hand, using embroidery thread. When complete, trim to size and stitch the embroidered white felt to the lower half of the small gingham square, then stitch both to the centre of the pink felt square. Machine stitch the pink felt square to the centre of the bag front.

MAKING A BASIC BAG

- Cut out two fabric rectangles to the required size, adding a 2cm seam allowance all round.
- Neaten the top edge of each piece by turning a double 1cm hem to the wrong side, stitch in place.
- Make the drawstring channel: mark 5cm down from the top edge on both fabric pieces. Machine stitch a strip of binding across each fabric piece at this level, and neaten the tape ends.
- Make up the bag: with right sides together, stitch the side and base edges, taking a 2cm seam allowance. Leave an opening in the side seams at the bindings, to create the drawstring channel opening. Neaten all raw edges, trim and press. Turn bag right side out.
- Add the cords: thread one cord through the channel and stitch the ends together securely. Repeat for the second cord. Pull up the cords on each side of the bag, ensuring that the cord joins are hidden inside the channel.

Colour-coded shoe bags

The colours can help you to identify the contents.

1 Making the bags These bags are all made following the basic bag instructions (page 64).

2 Decorating the bags Add coloured, embroidery thread knots randomly over the bag. To do this, make a small stitch through the fabric, then tie a double knot and trim off the ends. Cut a matching coloured felt scrap into an interesting shape, wrap around the cord knot and stick the ends together.

FOR EACH BAG
YOU WILL NEED

80 x 30cm wide cream fabric • **65 x 2.5cm wide matching bias binding** • 100cm thick cream cord • **coloured embroidery threads** • 12 x 6cm orange, green and blue scraps of felt • **fabric adhesive, we used Uhu All-Purpose Clear Adhesive** • matching sewing threads

Lacy bags

The two small bags shown left are made out of a lacy place-mat and a handkerchief. They are ideal for holding fragrant soap, pot pourri or dried lavender.

YOU WILL NEED

12cm square lace-edged handkerchief • **40cm square lace-edged place-mat** • 34cm x 5mm wide ribbon, for the small bag • **84 x 1cm wide ribbon, for the larger bag** • 46 x 1.5cm wide matching bias binding • **matching sewing threads**

1 Making the drawstring channels Make three pleats down the handkerchief and the place mat and tack in place. This converts the squares into rectangles. Measure and mark 4cm from the top and bottom edges of the handkerchief, and 8cm from the top and bottom of the place-mat. Machine stitch a strip of bias binding across the pleated fabric at these levels to form the drawstring channels and neaten the ends.

2 Making the bags Fold the fabric in half so the cord channels are level and machine stitch around the three sides of each bag, starting and ending just below the binding and securing the pleats across the base. Remove the tacking threads, then cut each ribbon into two equal lengths and thread through the bags.

Take one plain lampshade (left) and decorate! This is exactly what we have done to create these amazing table lampshades that will look great in any room. Original and exciting lampshades cost a fortune to buy, but it's quick and easy to decorate a plain ready-made shade to stunning effect and it doesn't have to cost a lot.

If you are artistic you can conjure up your own creative designs, or for inspiration you can copy these or others that you see in the shops. The great advantage of decorating your own shade is that you can create the design, and exactly match the colour to existing furnishings in a room.

decorative
lampshades

For all these decorative lampshades we used an inexpensive plain cream 30cm shade and, unless otherwise stated, we used PVA adhesive which dries clear. If you have a glue gun, this will be perfect for fixing on buttons and beads.

The marabou hat

YOU WILL NEED

3m length marabou fur ·
adhesive (optional) · needle
and matching thread

1 Stick or stitch one end of the
fur to the shade, 1cm down
from the top edge. To prevent
any risk of a fire hazard (see
Safety First Box page 69),
ensure that the top opening of
the shade is left completely clear.

2 Wrap the fur around the
shade and secure halfway
down with more glue or a stitch,
then continue to wrap the fur
around the shade.

3 Finish by securing the end
with a stitch or adhesive
along the lower edge.

The basket-weave

YOU WILL NEED

scalpel · **brown garden twine** · 3 types of textured paper in toning colours, (we used corrugated, twisted and recycled light brown paper) cut into strips

1 Measure and mark 16 equally spaced points around the top and base of the shade, centring one above the other. Using the scalpel, vertically slash the shade between the points to make 16 strips.

2 Weave the twine and strips of paper alternately through the shade. Overlap the paper ends and hide the joins. Tie the twine ends into bows.

The ethnic fringe

YOU WILL NEED

hole punch · **brown paper leatherette** · adhesive · **selection of small beads and shells and ivory-coloured elephant and fish earring ornaments** · natural-coloured raffia cut into 24cm lengths · **green paper wire ties**

1 Measure and mark 11 equally spaced points around the base of the shade and punch a hole at each point.

2 Tear up the leatherette paper into interesting-shaped pieces and stick them around the shade.

3 Stick the shells, beads and ornaments randomly over the shade.

4 Thread the raffia strips through the punched holes and secure in place with the wire ties.

The stamp collection

YOU WILL NEED

hole punch • **3m black leather thong** • adhesive • **selection of interesting used stamps** • light brown varnish and brush

1 Measure and mark eight equally spaced points around the top of the shade and 18 points around the base. Punch a hole at each point.

2 Thread the thong through the holes, knotting neatly at each end to secure.

3 Stick the stamps randomly over the shade, then apply the varnish evenly over the shade. Leave to dry thoroughly before use.

The floral bouquet

YOU WILL NEED

selection of large colourful silk flowers • **adhesive**

1 Remove the flowers from their stems and stick them over the lampshade, ensuring that the petals stand away from and leave the top opening of the shade clear.

SAFETY FIRST Use only the correct wattage light bulb recommended for the lampshade and ensure that the decoration is a safe distance from the top opening of the shade and the light bulb. The bulb should be at least 3cm away from the inside of the shade. Be very careful that it does not come within this recommended distance, or scorching and fire may occur. A fabric stiffener and flame-retardant spray by Carousel is available from John Lewis.

Interesting and unusual frames can bring out the best in the most simple pictures. Working on a nautical theme, we have taken plain frames and decorated them, some with beachcombing treasures, to complement picture postcards.

If you can't find suitable frames you can make them very easily and cheaply using balsa wood. To make a 20cm square frame with a 10cm square window, cut a 60cm length of 2 x 5cm wide balsa wood into four 15cm pieces. Using impact adhesive, stick them together to form a frame. When dry, fix a picture hanging hook to the back and the frame is ready for decorating. Once decorated, your picture can be stuck to the back of the frame with tape.

picture *frames*

Drifting by (*opposite, top*)
Cut thoroughly dried driftwood into suitable lengths. Spread a flat picture frame liberally with glue, then position the pieces with the cut edges of the driftwood parallel with the centre edge of the frame.

Drifting by (top), Gilt-edged (bottom left), Star turn (bottom right)

Gilt-edged

You can use any shaped moulds to make this frame design.

YOU WILL NEED

2.5kg bag plaster of Paris · **shell-shaped chocolate moulds** · sandpaper · **flat picture frame, or make a 20cm square frame (page 70)** · impact adhesive, such as Evo-stik · **cream acrylic paint and paint brush** · gold finger gilding paste · **white spirit, for cleaning your finger**

1 Making the plaster shells Add 150ml of plaster of Paris to 75ml of water and mix to the consistency of single cream. Pour into the moulds and leave to set for one hour. Turn out and leave to dry. Sand off any rough edges.

2 Creating the frame design Position the shells on the frame, then carefully stick in place. Leave to dry overnight. Coat with cream paint and leave to dry.

3 Adding a touch of gold Using your finger, rub a little of the gilding paste over visible areas of the frame and the shells.

HINTS & TIPS

• Bags of ice-lolly sticks, plaster of Paris and gold finger paste are available from Homecraft Direct (0116 2513139).

• Bags of plaster of Paris also available from chemists.

• Set of shell chocolate moulds from Squires Kitchen (01252 711749).

Star turn

YOU WILL NEED

card and double-sided tape · **flat picture frame, or make a 25cm square balsa wood frame with a 10cm square opening, using 7.5cm wide wood (page 70)** · 2.5kg bag plaster of Paris · **non-drying modelling clay, such as Playdough** · star cutter · sandpaper · ivory and pale blue acrylic paint and paint brush

1 Making the mould Cut four cardboard strips 25 x 7.5cm and, using double-sided tape, stick them vertically around the outside edge of the frame to form a 'box'. Cut another four cardboard strips 10 x 7.5cm and stick them around the edges of the centre opening in the same way. Now tape the card together at each 'box' corner to create a solid mould for the plaster.

2 Shaping the starfish Make eight starfish, each 1cm thick, from the modelling clay. You can use a star cutter for the basic shape, then finish by hand. Position around the frame and press gently into place.

3 Making the plaster frame Add a mug (about 300ml) of plaster of Paris to half a mug (about 150ml) of water and mix to the consistency of single cream. Pour into the frame mould so that the starfish just stand proud. Leave to set overnight.

4 Decorating the frame Remove the starfish which will have made indented motifs. Peel off the card and tape and sand any sharp edges. Cover the frame with the ivory coloured paint and leave to dry. When dry, use the blue to coat everything except the indented starfish.

Stuck on you

During the holidays ice-lolly sticks can be collected by the dozen, or you can buy them by the bag.

YOU WILL NEED

flat picture frame, or make a 18cm square balsa wood frame with a 10cm square opening, using 4cm wide wood (page 70) • **white and blue acrylic paint and paint brush** • 26 wooden ice-lolly sticks (more for a wider frame) • **hacksaw or craft knife** • sandpaper • **double-sided tape (optional)** • impact adhesive, such as Evo-stik

1 Preparing the frame If necessary, paint the frame white or blue to match the sticks.

2 Preparing the ice-lolly sticks Cut all the lolly sticks in half and sand the cut edges. Now paint half the sticks blue and half white. This is easy to do if you secure the sticks on double-sided tape while painting. Leave to dry.

3 Decorating the frame Cover the surface of the frame with adhesive then, using the picture as a guide, fix the sticks in place making sure that the cut edges are parallel with the inside edge of the frame. Leave to dry then, if necessary, touch up the paint on the sticks.

Pebble dash

Water-worn slate and small, flat pebbles can be found in country streams as well as along our coast. Choose pieces that match the size of your frame.

YOU WILL NEED

grey acrylic paint and paint brush • **flat picture frame, or make a 20cm square frame (page 70)** • small pebbles with a flat side • **small pieces of smooth slate** • impact adhesive, such as Evo-stik • **clear varnish (optional)**

1 Preparing the frame Paint the frame grey and leave to dry completely.

2 Creating the design Arrange the pebbles and slate to cover as much of the frame as possible – the flat slate can be overlapped. One at a time, lift each piece of slate or pebble, spread the underside with adhesive and reposition. Leave to dry overnight. For a sparkling wet look, varnish the pebbles and frame.

Who could have guessed that these beautiful plates and bowls were made from yesterday's newsprint? Papier mâché is yet another craft that gives you something for nothing – but it does require a little patience. The thickness and quality of the finished item depends on building up layer upon layer of paper. And it's essential that it dries thoroughly before being removed from the mould so that it keeps its shape. Almost any shaped plate or container can be reproduced in papier mâché, but wide brimmed bowls and plates are the easiest.

Papier mâché on a spherical object, like the jug in the picture, would have to be cut through with a knife to remove it from its mould, rather like a peach from its stone. The two halves are then pasted back together.

papier *mâché* bowls

Decoration adds a personal finishing touch. If you find painting motifs difficult, use a stencil or cut out paper motifs and stick them to the surface before protecting with coats of varnish.

You will need

bowl or plate to use as a mould • **Vaseline** • plastic film • **wallpaper paste** • newspaper • **scissors** • paste brush • **sharp craft knife** • paint brushes • **white emulsion** • pencil • **poster paints or emulsion paint sample pots in colours to suit your design** • clear poster paint varnish spray

1 Getting started Choose a bowl or plate shape you would like to reproduce. Cover the inside surface with Vaseline, then line with plastic film. Leave excess film hanging over the rim of the bowl to allow for easy removal when dry. Make up the wallpaper paste according to the instructions and roughly tear the newspaper into 5cm squares.

2 Applying the papier mâché Coat the plastic film with paste and apply an overlapping layer of pasted newspaper squares; continue until there are five layers of paper. Leave to dry overnight in a warm cupboard. Repeat each day until the papier mâché bowl or plate is the required thickness. Ensure that the last layer is as smooth as possible.

3 Removing the paper bowl or plate Leave the papier mâché to harden in a warm place for several days. If it is not thoroughly dry, the papier mâché will not keep its shape once removed from the mould. Carefully lift the overhanging edges of the plastic film and remove from the mould. Peel the plastic film from the underside of the bowl or plate.

4 Neatening the rim It may be necessary to trim the top edge to make it level. You can do this using either scissors or a craft knife, but you will need to be careful to avoid cutting too much off. When you are satisfied that the edge is straight, cover the rim with one smooth layer of pasted newspaper squares and leave overnight or longer until thoroughly dry.

5 Painting the bowl Paint the bowl or plate, both inside and out, with two coats of white emulsion – this will mask the newsprint and create a smooth surface for your decoration. Paint on at least one coat of your chosen coloured paint to achieve the desired background for your design. Leave to dry thoroughly between each coat of paint.

6 Adding the design Plan your design and draw on to the bowl or plate. Alternatively, trace the flower design shown, then paint on the colours. If you can't draw or paint, colour photocopy our design and use wall-paper paste to stick in place. You may need to enlarge or reduce it and make a number of copies. Leave to dry.

7 Finishing touch When dry, two applications of clear varnish spray will protect and add the finishing touch to your papier mâché.

Everyone needs a little help to keep everyday clutter under control. These pretty boxes are great for storing 101 notoriously difficult things from socks to disorganized cassettes and treasured photos, and best of all they cost next to nothing. In fact, the boxes are free – they are shoe boxes that shops are happy to give away. We simply covered them in colour co-ordinating fabrics.

Shoe boxes come in several sizes, so start by finding boxes that suit whatever you want to store, then choose fabrics that match the colour and style of your room. Thinner fabrics rather than heavy-duty furnishing fabrics are best because they wrap around the corners more easily, and try to avoid fabrics that fray. The cheapest options, of course, are fabric remnants.

shoe *box* storage

YOU WILL NEED

shoe boxes in several sizes · **80 x 112cm wide fabric, or 50 x 150cm wide fabric for an average sized box** · spray adhesive, such as spray mount · **fabric adhesive – we used Uhu All Purpose Clear Adhesive** · double-sided iron-on bonding material, such as Bondaweb · **scissors** · card for box dividers, lid and floor

1 Measuring up the box Following the diagram, measure the circumference of the box, A and the inside and outside height of the box walls, B. Cut out a rectangle of fabric to these measurements, adding 2cm all round to allow for fabric turnings.

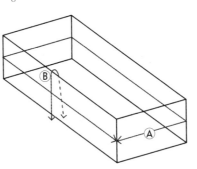

2 Covering the outside walls Working on each outside wall in turn, spray the box side with adhesive and smooth the fabric over to cover it. Position the fabric with the 2cm seam allowance at the first corner and along the base edge. Work around the box, finishing where you started. Turn under raw edges to match the corner edges, then stick them in place with fabric adhesive. Stick the seam allowance to the underside of the box.

3 Covering the inside walls Turn the box on to its base and spray adhesive around the inside box walls. Smooth the fabric over the top edge on to each of the walls in turn, forming neat corners and sticking the seam allowance on to the inner box floor.

4 Neatening the base Draw the box base on to the paper backing of the bonding material. Cut out, adding 1cm allowance all round. Iron this to the wrong side of the fabric. Cut out the fabric rectangle, 5mm inside the drawn box line. Peel off the paper backing, centre the fabric on the box base and iron in place.

(Continued at the top of page 81.)

5 Covering the box floor Cut out a piece of card to fit the floor of the box. Then cut out a piece of fabric to this size, adding 2cm allowance all round. Spray one side of the card with adhesive, centre over the wrong side of the fabric and stick in place. Using fabric adhesive, stick the fabric allowance to the back of the card. Fit into box.

6 Covering the lid Following the diagram above, measure the box lid, C and D. Cut out a rectangle of fabric to this measurement, adding 2cm allowance all round. Spray top of lid and stick centrally to the wrong side of fabric. Using the fabric adhesive, stick the fabric to the outside and inside walls of the lid, taking care to neaten the corners. Neaten the inside of the lid as for the box floor.

HINTS & TIPS

- Use light fabrics.

- If the fabric has a tendency to fray, cut it out with pinking shears – alternatively, you can bond the fabric to a fine interfacing before cutting it out.

- You should always test adhesive and bonding materials on the fabric before use to check for staining.

- If the fabric remnants you buy are too small to cover an entire box, you can cover the lid in a co-ordinating fabric.

- If you wish to cover several boxes in co-ordinating fabrics, buy fabrics off the roll.

- The boxes can be covered in paper using exactly the same method, but the covers will be less durable.

Making the box dividers

If you wish to divide up the interior of the box, you need to cut out card dividers and cover them with fabric. The number of dividers depends on how many compartments you need.

1 Measuring up Cut out the box dividers from strips of card. The strip length should be cut to match the inside dimensions of the box. The height of the card strip should be at least 1cm less than the depth of the box.

2 Covering with fabric Cut out a rectangle of fabric the same length and twice the width of each card divider – no allowance is needed. Spray one side of the card with adhesive, stick to the wrong side of the fabric matching three edges. Spray the other side of the card with adhesive, fold the fabric over and smooth in place.

3 Fitting together Following the diagram below, measure and mark the compartment length along the base edge of the lengthways dividers, then make a vertical cut at each point – from the base edge to halfway up. Measure and mark the compartment width along the top edge of the widthways dividers, then make a vertical cut from the top edge to halfway down the dividers. Slot together and place in the box. The boxes are now ready to be filled with your chosen knick-knacks.

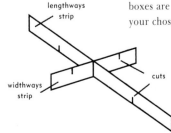

lengthways strip

widthways strip

cuts

cooking
for
special
occasions

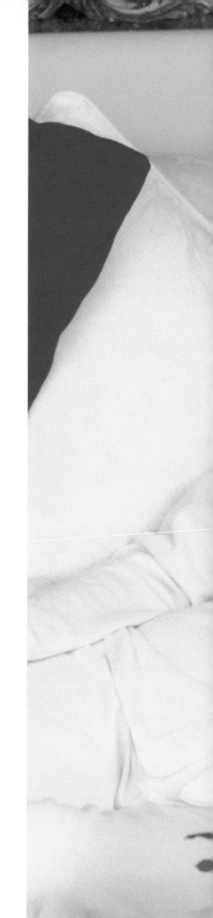

I love celebrating special occasions and inviting family and friends to join us. As with most people, my entertaining has become more and more casual over the years but I do spend quite a lot of time planning the menu and deciding how each dish will be served – it can save a last-minute panic. Here are some of my favourite recipes for four very different occasions: a spring wedding, a summer lunch, a Hallowe'en party and a Christmas drinks get-together.

Deciding to prepare a celebration meal, such as a wedding breakfast for twenty people or more, can feel a little daunting, but it can be done very successfully with careful planning, organization and help. I always think it's important to remember that preparing the meal is probably just one item of many on your agenda for the special day. There may be tables to be laid, flowers to do and, most importantly, you will want to enjoy the party, too. Arrange to have lots of help on the day – ideally you should plan to do nothing other than to organize and advise. Be sure to leave at least an hour to relax and dress for the party.

spring *wedding*

MENU

Courgette and peppercorn terrine
•
Spiced glazed salmon
Coriander and mango mayonnaise
Marinated cucumber salad
Duck and turkey pie
Pine nut and Parmesan strudel
Couscous niçoise
•
Lemon syllabub trifle
Pear and raspberry compote with cinnamon cream

TIME PLAN

Make and freeze ahead
Duck and turkey pie
Pine nut and Parmesan strudel
•
Two days before
Make Courgette and peppercorn terrine
Make Duck and turkey pie, or thaw if frozen
Make Lemon syllabub trifle up to stage 4
Make Pear and raspberry compote
•
One day before
Cook salmon
Thaw and cook Pine nut and Parmesan Strudel
Make Marinated cucumber salad
Make Couscous niçoise
Complete Lemon syllabub trifle
•
On the day
Dress the salmon
Turn out Courgette and peppercorn terrine
Garnish and decorate all dishes

Clockwise from left:
Couscous niçoise, Pine nut and Parmesan strudel,
Coriander and mango mayonnaise,
Duck and turkey pie, Lemon syllabub trifle,
Marinated cucumber salad, Spiced glazed salmon

Courgette and peppercorn terrine

This is not suitable for freezing, but can be made up to two days in advance.

Serves 20

4 tbsp olive oil
675g/1 1/2 lb small courgettes
2 tbsp powdered gelatine
4 tbsp white wine vinegar
675g/1 1/2 lb mascarpone cheese, at room
  temperature
40g/1 1/2 oz pink peppercorns, drained and crushed
  or chopped
675g/1 1/2 lb plum tomatoes, skinned, halved and
  cut into chunky pieces
25g/1oz fresh basil (stalks removed), chopped
150ml/1/4 pint double cream
salt and freshly ground black pepper
fresh basil leaves, to garnish

1 Preheat the oven to 200C/400F/Gas 6. Lightly oil two 450g/1lb loaf tins and line with plastic film. Cover a large baking sheet with foil and oil lightly.
2 Thinly slice two-thirds of the courgettes lengthways and place on the baking sheet. Brush with olive oil and season. Bake for 20 minutes or until beginning to colour. Cool.
3 Grate the remaining courgettes and sprinkle with plenty of salt. Leave for 30 minutes, then rinse thoroughly and squeeze dry.
4 Arrange half the courgette slices, overlapping, in the tin bases. Sprinkle the gelatine over the vinegar in a small bowl and leave for 5 minutes. Reserve 115g/4oz of mascarpone, then beat the remainder to soften. Stir in the peppercorns, basil, tomatoes and grated courgettes; season with salt.
5 Bring the cream and the reserved mascarpone just to the boil. Stir in the gelatine and heat gently until dissolved. Stir into the cheese mixture.
6 Spoon half the mixture over the courgettes, level the surfaces. Cover with courgette slices, add the remaining cheese mixture. Cover and chill.
7 Invert the tins on to a flat plate and peel away the film. Serve thinly sliced garnished with basil.

Spiced glazed salmon

Order the salmon about a week in advance and ask the fishmonger to clean it for you. You can serve one 2.7kg/6lb salmon or two 1.3-1.8kg/3-4lb salmon and cook one at a time. Before cooking, check the salmon fits in the oven. You may find you have to bake it diagonally, removing the head if it is too long. If so, bake this in a separate piece of foil so that you can use it for presentation. Alternatively, cook a large salmon in a fish kettle. Bake a day in advance; glaze and garnish on the wedding morning as shown above right.

Serves 20

oil, for brushing
2.7kg/6lb whole salmon
2 limes
small handful fresh coriander
1 tsp ground coriander
5 tbsp strained mango chutney
salt and freshly ground black pepper
fresh coriander or flatleaf parsley and lime
  wedges, to garnish
Coriander and mango mayonnaise, to serve
  (recipe above right)

1 Preheat the oven to 190C/375F/Gas 5. Lay a piece of foil, slightly more than twice the length of the salmon, on the work surface and brush with a little oil. Place the salmon at one end. Season the cavity with salt and pepper. Cut one lime into small pieces and tuck into the cavity with the fresh coriander.

2 Bring the remaining foil over the salmon and seal the edges together so that there is an air pocket around the fish. Lift on to a baking sheet and bake for 10 minutes per 450g/1lb. Remove from the oven and leave to cool.

3 Carefully turn over the salmon. Using the tip of a knife, cut through the skin along the back of the salmon, around the head, and across the tail. Gently peel away the skin. Invert the salmon on to a serving platter and then peel away the skin on this side.

4 Mix together the ground coriander, mango chutney and one tablespoon of lime juice from one of the limes and chill. Cover the salmon loosely and chill overnight.

5 Brush the salmon with the mango glaze. Garnish and serve with the Coriander and mango mayonnaise.

Coriander and mango mayonnaise

Make the mayonnaise a day in advance and then chill overnight.

Serves 20

1 ripe mango, skinned, halved, stoned and flesh
  grated
425ml/³/4 pint mayonnaise
150ml/¹/4 pint crème fraîche
grated rind of 3 limes
6 tbsp chopped fresh coriander
4 tbsp chopped fresh parsley
salt and freshly ground black pepper

1 Mix together all the ingredients. Cover and chill until needed.

Marinated cucumber salad

Make this a day in advance, stirring in the mangetout on the morning.

Serves 20

400g/14oz mangetout or sugar snap peas
3 large cucumbers, peeled, halved lengthways,
  seeded and cut diagonally
2 tbsp mustard seeds
2 small red onions, finely chopped
115g/4oz caperberries (about ¹/2 jar), or 55g/2oz
  capers in brine, drained
4 tbsp fresh lemon juice
4 tsp caster sugar
salt and freshly ground black pepper

1 Blanch the mangetout or sugar snap peas in boiling water for 1 minute, drain and plunge into cold water immediately to refresh. Place the cucumbers in a large bowl.

2 Heat the mustard seeds in a pan until they pop. Cool slightly, then add to the cucumbers with the red onions and caperberries.

3 Mix together the lemon juice and sugar and spoon over the salad. Season lightly, cover and chill overnight.

4 Stir in the mangetout or sugar snap peas and transfer to serving dishes.

Duck and turkey pie

Although time-consuming to prepare, this pie can be made two days in advance or frozen for up to a month. Transfer from the freezer to the fridge 48 hours before serving.

Serves 20

700g/1lb 9oz plain flour
1 tsp salt
225g/8oz white vegetable fat, cubed
1 egg yolk

FOR THE TURKEY LAYER

900g/2lb minced turkey
1 small onion, chopped
85g/3oz shelled pistachios
1 tsp salt
freshly ground black pepper
1 tbsp chopped fresh oregano
200g/7oz streaky bacon rashers

FOR THE DUCK LAYER

2 skinless duck breasts, cut into strips
115g/4oz dried apples or pears, sliced
2 tsp powdered gelatine
300ml/1/2 pint chicken stock

1 Make the pastry: sift the flour and salt into a bowl. Place the fat in a pan with 225ml/8fl oz water. Heat gently until the fat has melted. Bring to the boil and immediately tip in the flour. Beat with a wooden spoon until the mixture forms a smooth dough. Cover while preparing the filling.
2 Mix together the turkey, onion, pistachios, seasoning and oregano.
3 Preheat the oven to 200C/400F/Gas 6. Lightly grease a 23cm/9in round spring-release tin. Reserve a third of the pastry. Roll out remainder and use to line the base and sides of the tin, letting a little excess pastry come over the rim. Mould around the side to remove any cracks.
4 Spoon a quarter of the turkey mixture into the base of the tin and cover with half the bacon rashers. Spoon another quarter of the turkey mixture over the bacon.
5 Arrange the duck strips in a spiral over the turkey, working from the side into the centre, and leaving a gap between the strips for the apples or pears. Fill the gaps with the fruit.
6 Spread with another quarter of the turkey mixture, then the remaining bacon and turkey mixture, doming slightly in the centre. Mix the egg yolk with one tablespoon of water and brush a little around the pastry rim.
7 Roll out the remaining pastry to form a lid. Trim off the excess pastry with a knife and crimp the edges to decorate. Make a hole in the centre of the pie and brush the top with egg yolk. Make leaves from the pastry trimmings and place around the centre hole.
8 Bake the pie for 15 minutes, then reduce the oven temperature to 180C/350F/Gas 4. Bake for a further 2 hours, covering the pie with foil if it starts to over-brown. Carefully remove the side of the tin and brush all round the pie with egg yolk. Bake for another 15 minutes. Leave to cool completely.
9 Sprinkle the gelatine over two tablespoons of water in a bowl and leave for 5 minutes. Heat the stock and stir in the gelatine until dissolved. Leave until cool, but not set. Pour into the pie through the hole in the centre; you may find it easier to use a funnel. Chill the pie overnight.

Pine nut and Parmesan strudel

Freeze the uncooked strudel on a baking sheet up to a month in advance, then cook the day before the wedding. Or, freeze cooked, and simply crisp in a hot oven for 10-15 minutes on the morning.

Serves 10

115g/4oz white bread, diced
8 tbsp olive oil
1 large onion, chopped
200g/7oz pine nuts
2 celery sticks, sliced
2 garlic cloves, crushed
250g/9oz ricotta
55g/2oz grated Parmesan
6 tbsp roughly chopped fresh parsley
12 sheets filo pastry
salt and freshly ground black pepper
flatleaf parsley, celery leaves and Parmesan
   shavings, to garnish

1 Preheat the oven to 190C/375F/Gas 5. Fry the cubes of bread in three tablespoons of the oil until golden. Drain. Add three more tablespoons of oil to the pan and fry the onion and pine nuts until golden.

2 Stir in the celery and garlic and fry for a further 2 minutes. Turn into a bowl with the bread and add the ricotta, Parmesan and parsley. Season and stir until evenly combined.
3 Lay two sheets of filo pastry, overlapping slightly, on the work surface. Brush lightly with a little of the remaining oil. Lay two more sheets over the first so the overlapping join goes in the opposite direction.
4 Spread half the filling across the pastry in a sausage, about 5cm/2in away from one end. Roll up, bend into a semi-circle and transfer to a baking sheet. Repeat with four more pastry sheets and the remaining filling. Position on the sheet to make a ring, pressing the ends firmly together.
5 Brush the ring with oil. Crumple the remaining sheets of pastry and arrange over the ring, tucking the ends underneath. Brush with oil and bake for 30-40 minutes until golden. Leave to cool, then chill or freeze.
6 Fill the centre with parsley and celery leaves. Scatter with Parmesan shavings.

Couscous niçoise

Serves 20

300g/10½ oz French beans
450g/1lb couscous
300g/10½ oz radishes, sliced
500g/1lb 2oz cherry tomatoes, halved
115g/4oz pitted black olives
225ml/8fl oz olive oil
50ml/2fl oz white wine vinegar
2 garlic cloves, crushed
salt and freshly ground black pepper

1 Cook the beans in boiling water for 2 minutes until just tender. Drain and refresh in cold water.
2 Place the couscous in a large bowl with 600ml/1pint boiling water. Leave for 5 minutes, then fluff up with a fork to separate the grains.
3 Stir in the beans, radishes, tomatoes and olives. Mix the oil with the vinegar, garlic and plenty of seasoning. Add to the salad and chill overnight. Stir lightly and transfer to serving dishes.

Lemon syllabub trifle

Complete up to the end of step 4 two days in advance, ready for adding the syllabub cream the following day.

Serves 15

225g/8oz caster sugar
6 lemons
two shop-bought Madeira cakes, each about
  250g/9oz, cut into small pieces
6 tbsp gin or vodka
225g/8oz lemon curd
1 litre/1¾ pints double cream

1 Heat the sugar in a heavy-based pan with 600ml/1 pint water until the sugar dissolves. Bring to the boil and boil for 2 minutes.
2 Using a sharp knife, pare strips from three of the lemons and reserve. Cut away the skin from all the lemons and slice the flesh, discarding any of the pips.
3 Add the lemon slices and pared rind to the syrup and simmer gently for about 10 minutes until the lemon slices are tender but just keeping their shape. Drain, reserving the syrup.
4 Place the Madeira cake pieces in the base of a glass serving dish. Add the lemon slices, pressing some against the sides of the glass. Reserve half the syrup. Stir the gin or, if preferred, vodka into the remainder of the syrup and pour over the sponge.
5 Blend the lemon curd with the remaining syrup. Place the cream in a large bowl with the lemon curd and syrup mixture and stir until thickened. If it takes a little while, use an electric whisk, but take care not to over-whisk or the texture will be spoilt.
6 When just thickened, spoon over the trifle. Pile up the reserved lemon rind in the centre and then chill overnight.

Lemon syllabub trifle (top) and
Pear and raspberry compote (below)

Pear and raspberry compote with cinnamon cream

This can be made and chilled one to two days in advance of the occasion.

Serves 12

175g/6oz caster sugar
1 bottle Beaujolais
12 firm pears
250g/9oz fresh or frozen raspberries
4 tbsp raspberry vinegar
fresh bay leaves, to decorate

FOR THE CINNAMON CREAM
200ml/7fl oz crème fraîche
150ml/¼ pint double cream
1 tbsp icing sugar, sifted
1 tsp ground cinnamon

1 Heat the sugar with the Beaujolais wine in a large, heavy-based pan until the sugar has completely dissolved.
2 Using a sharp knife, take a thin slice off the base of the pears, if necessary, so that they stand upright in the pan and on the serving plate. Peel the pears, leaving them whole with their stalks attached. Alternatively, you may prefer to leave the skins on and use a citrus peeler to cut decorative grooves.
3 Pack the pears into the wine syrup in the pan and cook very gently for 15-25 minutes until softened. This will depend on the firmness of the pears. Transfer to a large bowl.
4 Add half the raspberries to the syrup with the raspberry vinegar. Bring to the boil and boil until reduced and slightly thickened. Strain over the pears and leave to cool. Stir in the remaining raspberries and chill for one to two days.
5 Make the cinnamon cream: beat together the crème fraîche, cream, icing sugar and cinnamon and transfer to a serving dish.
6 Stand the pears on a large serving plate and spoon over the syrup and raspberries. Decorate with the fresh bay leaves and serve with the cinnamon cream.

I love having friends round for lunch – usually on a Sunday. I find it easier to spend time in the kitchen at weekends, when the pressures of work, helping with homework and everyday family meals is off. The main dish from this lunch party menu, Saffron salmon pie with chive cream sauce is a great favourite of mine. It's really quite easy to make, using ready prepared pastry, yet looks very impressive and is absolutely delicious. The Parmesan and garlic toasts are also handy, make them any time, cook and store in the freezer. This summer lunch is the sort of meal you can eat *al fresco* on a sunny day or enjoy inside if the weather turns chilly.

summer
lunch party

Parmesan garlic toasts

These quick and easy home-made nibbles are ideal for whetting the appetite. I serve them with drinks as I welcome my guests.

Serves 6-8

6 thick slices of white bread, crusts removed
50g/1³/₄ oz garlic butter softened
50g/1³/₄ oz Parmesan, finely grated

1 Preheat the oven to 200C/400F/Gas 6. Roll bread slices with a rolling pin until very flat. Cut four circles from each slice, using a 6cm/ 2½ in plain or fluted cutter. Place on baking sheets.
2 Spread with garlic butter and sprinkle with Parmesan. Bake for 10 minutes or until the Parmesan is melted and golden.

TIP

Open freeze the cooked toasts on trays, then pack into a sealed container. Reheat from frozen for 5-6 minutes.

Right: Avocado and watercress soup

Shown on page 95:
Golden saffron salmon pie with Minted pesto potatoes and Julienne vegetable salad

Avocado and watercress soup

Chilled soups make a perfect summer starter. I love this one with its creamy texture and tangy flavour. Serve with jazzed up ready-to-bake rolls. Brush with beaten egg and sprinkle with caraway, poppy or sesame seeds, then bake the rolls according to instructions on the packet.

Serves 8

25g/1oz butter
1 tbsp vegetable or olive oil
2 medium onions, finely chopped
2 garlic cloves, crushed
2 x 75g bags watercress
1.4 litres/2¹/₂ pints good chicken or vegetable stock
3 ripe avocados, preferably Hass
150ml/¹/₄ pint soured cream
juice of 1 lemon (about 4 tbsp)
seasoning

FOR THE GARNISH

1 red pepper
1¹/₂ tbsp virgin olive oil
fresh coriander leaves
freshly ground black pepper

1 Melt the butter with the oil in a large pan. Add the onions and garlic and gently fry for 10 minutes until very soft, stirring occasionally. Stir in the watercress and 300ml/¹/₂ pint chicken stock and bring to the boil. Cook for 5 minutes, stirring occasionally, until the watercress is well wilted. Remove from the heat and cool for 5 minutes.
2 Spoon the onion mixture into a food processor and blend for 1 minute. Peel, stone and roughly chop avocados and add to the processor. Add the soured cream, lemon juice and seasoning and blend until smooth. Gradually add 600ml/1 pint stock and continue to blend for 30 seconds.
3 Transfer to a large bowl, add remaining stock and adjust seasoning. Place a piece of plastic film on the surface of the soup, making sure it is completely sealed from the air. Chill for 4-18 hours before spooning into bowls or hollowed out melon shells. This soup is best served after 4-5 hours but you can make it further ahead. The surface may go a little brown but you can either skim it off or stir it into the rest of the soup – it won't affect the flavour.
4 Before serving, make the garnish: grill the red pepper all over until the skin blisters and browns. Remove from the heat and place in a sealed plastic bag for 5 minutes – this softens the skin making it easier to peel. Peel off pepper skin, seed and finely slice. Arrange strips of the pepper on to each bowl of soup, drizzle with virgin olive oil, then top with coriander and ground black pepper, and serve.

Golden saffron salmon pie with chive cream sauce

I find ready-rolled puff pastry very convenient and easy to use, but don't worry if your local shops don't stock it. Use 2 x 250g/9oz puff pastry blocks instead and roll out to 3mm/¹/₈ in thick. Use leftover pastry for decorations.

Serves 6-8

2 tbsp vegetable oil
6 spring onions, finely sliced
175g/6oz basmati rice, well rinsed
350ml/12fl oz vegetable stock
250ml/9fl oz dry white wine
good pinch saffron strands
200ml carton coconut cream
juice of ¹/₂ lemon
3 tbsp chopped fresh coriander
15g/¹/₂ oz butter
225g/8oz young spinach leaves
2 x 375g ready-rolled puff pastry sheets, thawed
    if frozen
800g/1³/₄ lb whole thick fresh salmon fillet,
    skinned
25g/1oz ground almonds
1 egg, beaten
seasoning
fresh coriander sprigs, to garnish

FOR THE SAUCE

250ml/9fl oz dry white wine
400ml/14fl oz double cream
4 tbsp snipped fresh chives

1 Heat the oil in a large pan and gently fry the onions and rice for 1 minute, stirring. Stir in the stock, wine and saffron. Bring to the boil, reduce the heat and simmer gently for about 15 minutes, stirring regularly.

2 Stir in the coconut cream and continue cooking until all the liquid is absorbed and the rice is creamy and tender. Season well, then stir in the lemon juice and coriander and leave to cool for 20 minutes.

3 Melt the butter in a large pan and stir fry the spinach for about 1 minute until wilted. Drain into a large sieve and press well with the back of a wooden spoon to squeeze out the excess liquid. Unroll one piece of the pastry and cut into a 30 x 15cm/12 x 6in rectangle, reserving trimmings. Place on a large baking tray or in a roasting tin.

4 Spread the rice over the pastry to within 2.5cm/1in of the edges. Top with the salmon, then cover with the spinach. Season and sprinkle with the ground almonds. Brush pastry edges with beaten egg. Cover with remaining puff pastry sheet and press edges together firmly to seal.

5 Use the trimmings to cut oval leaves, make a cone of pastry and overlap circles of pastry around to make a rose. Attach with beaten egg. Cover with plastic film and chill for 1-6 hours before baking.

6 Preheat the oven to 200C/400F/Gas 6. Brush pie with egg to glaze and bake for 45-50 minutes until puffed and golden. Serve warm or cold, garnished with fresh coriander sprigs.

7 Make the sauce: place the wine in a pan and bring to the boil. Simmer for 5-6 minutes until reduced to about 125ml/4fl oz. Add the cream and simmer again, stirring occasionally, for a further 6-8 minutes until the sauce begins to reduce and thicken, but take care that it doesn't boil over. Stir in the chives and season. Serve warm over slices of the pie.

Minted pesto potatoes

New potatoes have never tasted as good as these –
served warm with a deliciously pungent minted
pesto sauce. Make the pesto sauce up to three
days in advance. Spoon into a jar, cover and chill
until required.

Serves 6-8

1.5kg/3lb 5oz baby new potatoes

FOR THE PESTO

15g/¹/₂ oz fresh mint leaves
100g/3¹/₂ oz pine nuts
2 garlic cloves
125ml/4fl oz olive oil
50g/1³/₄ oz Parmesan, coarsely grated
1 tbsp fresh lemon juice
seasoning

1 Cook the potatoes in a pan of boiling salted
water for 12-15 minutes until tender. Meanwhile,
make the pesto: place the mint leaves, pine nuts,
garlic, oil, Parmesan, lemon juice and seasoning
in a food processor and blend for 1 minute.
2 Drain the potatoes, then return to the pan and
add the pesto. Toss really well and transfer to a
serving bowl.

Julienne vegetable salad with sweet and sour vinaigrette

Serves 6-8

150g/5¹/₂ oz red or white cabbage
*200g/7oz mooli (Chinese radish) or 100g/3¹/₂ oz
   small red radishes, sliced*
2 medium carrots
1 small red pepper, seeded
1 small yellow pepper, seeded
1 medium courgette

FOR THE DRESSING

4 tsp red wine vinegar
3 tbsp vegetable oil
1 tbsp mango chutney
¹/₄ tsp Chinese five-spice powder
seasoning

1 Make the dressing: place the ingredients in
screw-top jar and shake until well mixed. Adjust
the seasoning.
2 Finely shred all the vegetables, preferably with
a mandoline or the shredding disc of a food
processor. Place in a large serving bowl, cover and
chill for up to 8 hours. Toss with the dressing just
before serving.

Summer fruit jelly

This stunning dessert is much simpler to make
than it looks – make the most of your time by
assembling it while you are preparing other
dishes – it will take about 1½ hours.

Serves 6

450ml/16fl oz fresh orange juice
juice of 1 lemon
450ml/16fl oz cranberry juice drink
8 sheets leaf gelatine
2 large oranges, peeled and segmented
150g/5½ oz raspberries
150g/5½ oz small fresh strawberries, halved
2 nectarines, stoned and sliced
150g/5½ oz green or black seedless grapes
fresh strawberry and mint to decorate

1 Place the orange and lemon juice in one pan
and cranberry juice in another. Add four sheets of
gelatine, broken into halves, to each pan. Heat
juices without boiling, stirring, until the gelatine
has dissolved. Pour jellies into two jugs.
2 Rinse out a 1.4 litre/2½ pint metal mould with
cold water or line with plastic film. Pour a thin
layer of orange jelly over the base. Place in the
freezer until just set (do not freeze). Allow the
remaining jelly to cool but not set.
3 Arrange some of the orange segments on the
set jelly in the tin. Just cover with a little more
orange jelly, then return to the freezer until set.
Next, place a layer of raspberries and strawberries
on the orange jelly and just cover with some of
the cranberry jelly. Place in the freezer until just
set. Repeat layering and setting steps until all the
fruit and jelly is used, alternating orange and
cranberry jelly. If the unused jelly starts to set, just
heat gently in the pan until melted but not hot.
4 Cover tin with plastic film and chill until
completely set – up to 24 hours before serving. To
serve, dip mould into hot water for a few seconds.
Quickly turn out on to a plate and decorate.

Summer fruit jelly (far left)
Marbled white and dark chocolate mousse tart (left)

Marbled white and dark chocolate mousse tart

Makes 8-10 slices

FOR THE BASE
175g/6oz pecan nuts
100g/3½ oz butter, melted
175g/6oz plain flour
75g/2¾ oz light muscovado sugar

FOR THE FILLING
50g/1¾ oz cornflour
200ml/7fl oz milk
3 eggs, separated
150g/5½ oz plain chocolate, broken into squares
150g/5½ oz white chocolate, broken into squares
50g/1¾ oz caster sugar
icing sugar and cocoa powder, for dusting
lightly whipped cream or crème fraîche, to serve

1 Preheat the oven to 200C/400F/Gas 6. Finely
grind the pecan nuts. Stir in the butter, flour and
sugar and blend for 30 seconds. Press the mixture
evenly into the base and up the sides of a deep
23cm/9in fluted, loose-bottomed flan tin. Place on
a baking sheet and chill.
2 Make the filling: blend the cornflour with a
little milk in a pan until smooth. Stir in the rest of
the milk and heat very gently, stirring, until the
sauce begins to thicken. Beat in the egg yolks.
Divide the sauce between two bowls set over small
pans of simmering water.
3 Stir the plain chocolate into one bowl and the
white into the other. Heat until melted and the
sauces are thick and smooth, stirring regularly.
Remove and cool for 5 minutes.
4 Whisk the egg whites until stiff but not dry,
then gradually whisk in caster sugar. Fold half the
meringue into each chocolate mixture. Pour
alternate chocolate mixtures into the flan tin and
swirl lightly using a table knife. Bake for 30-35
minutes until well risen. Cool for 20 minutes,
then remove from tin. Serve warm or cover and
chill overnight. Dust with icing sugar and cocoa,
and serve with cream or crème fraîche.

You don't often have the opportunity to plan your entertaining to be as revolting, frightening and creepy as possible. Hallowe'en, though, is the perfect occasion for you and your family to dig deep into the depths of your imagination and just let go.

It used to be a tradition in our house to have a Hallowe'en party every year for the children and I have included a few of the games we used to play. I hope you and your friends have a thoroughly horrible time!

hallowe'en *party*

Hallowe'en party games

Dusty miller Half-fill a large bowl with flour and mix in six, well-scrubbed 50p pieces. Cover the floor with a plastic sheet and place the bowl in the centre. Players then kneel on the ground with their arms behind their backs and try to fish out as many coins as they can with their teeth. Some players will bury their faces in the flour and come up ghostly white, while wise guys will simply blow away the flour before picking up the coins with their teeth.

Eyeball salad, Meringue bones and Ghoul sticks.

Musical torchlight Players sit on the floor in a circle in a darkened room. One player is given a lighted torch and when the music plays it is passed around the group. To make the game as creepy as possible each player should hold the torch just below their chin and, while the music is playing, make ghostly noises. Whoever is holding the torch when the music stops is out.

The witch's story Before the party, prepare a tray of items that feel like parts of the body – peeled grapes for eyeballs, wet plastic film for skin, raw sausages for fingers, cooked spaghetti for veins, warm milk for blood and so on. An adult then dresses up as a witch and invites the children into a dark room to hear her story. The witch tells how she likes to eat juicy little children and how she has been lucky enough to catch one today. Would they like to feel some of the bits she is going to have for her dinner? Then she passes the nasty feeling bits around the group describing them as each child feels them. It's really spooky, but it's usually a very popular game with all ages.

Brimstone stew

It's fun to serve this in a large hollowed out water melon to imitate a cauldron.

Serves 6

175g/6oz spirals or other pasta shapes
115g/4oz tagliatelle verdi
450g/1lb pork sausages
2 tbsp oil
115g/4oz baby onions, peeled or 1 medium onion,
   chopped
250g/9oz pork mince
1 tsp mild chilli powder
2 x 400g cans chopped tomatoes
1 tsp caster sugar
300ml/1/2 pint chicken stock
1 red pepper, seeded and chopped
salt and pepper

1 Cook the pasta shapes in a large pan of boiling salted water until just tender. Drain and repeat for the tagliatelle.
2 Fry the sausages in the oil until browned. Remove the sausages, drain the oil, then add the onions, pork and chilli powder and fry gently for 3 minutes. Add the tomatoes, sugar and stock and return the sausages to the pan. Bring to the boil, reduce the heat and simmer gently for 30 minutes.
3 Season to taste, stir in the red pepper and pasta and simmer for 5 minutes to heat through.

'Eyeball' salad

Serves 4-8

1/2 crisp green lettuce
4 hard-boiled eggs, peeled and halved
pitted black olives, cut in half
3 tbsp tomato ketchup

1 Arrange the lettuce on a flat plate, top with egg halves, then place an olive on top of each egg. Place the ketchup in a piping bag fitted with a writer nozzle.
2 Pipe jagged lines of ketchup over the eggs and into the olive centres.

Grisly green mash

Serves 6

1.25kg/2³/4 lb potatoes
115g/4oz peas
dot of butter
115g/4oz Red Leicester cheese, thinly sliced
seasoning

1 Cook the potatoes in boiling salted water until tender, then drain. Cook the peas until tender, then drain. Blend until smooth, then mash into the potatoes with butter and season.
2 Cut out star or crescent shapes from the cheese slices and use to garnish the top of the mash.

Ghoul sticks

Makes 4

icing sugar, for dusting
handful of white mini-marshmallows
4 individual sponge fairy cakes
2 tbsp strawberry or raspberry jam
350g/12oz white ready-to-roll icing
4 liquorice 'bootlaces'
black paste food colouring

1 Dust four skewers with icing sugar, then thread marshmallows halfway up. Thread a fairy cake on to the top of each. Lay sticks on greaseproof paper. Melt the jam and brush over sponges.
2 Divide icing into four. Roll out one piece to a 20cm/8in round and brush lightly with water. Lay the sponge end of a stick on the icing, then bring the icing over the sponge and pinch the ends together. Transfer to a clean piece of paper. Repeat with remaining icing and cakes and leave to harden, preferably overnight.
3 Tie a piece of liquorice 'bootlace' around each stick and paint on eyes.

Gruesome jelly

Serves 6

1 lime flavoured jelly
2 lemon flavoured jellies
jelly snakes, spiders and small insects

1 Make up the jellies and mix together. Pour half into a 1.7 litre/3 pint glass serving dish and chill until lightly set.
2 Arrange the sweets over the jelly, pushing some into the jelly and around the sides so that they can be seen.
3 Ladle the remaining jelly mixture into the bowl and chill until set, then arrange more sweets over the jelly.

Meringue bones

Makes about 15

2 egg whites
115g/4oz caster sugar

1 Preheat the oven to 120C/250F/Gas 1/2. Line a large baking sheet with non-stick baking paper.
2 Whisk the egg whites until stiff. Whisk in the sugar, a tablespoon at a time, until stiff and glossy.
3 Place in a piping bag fitted with a 1cm/½in plain nozzle. Pipe 10-13cm/4-5in long meringue fingers on to the baking sheet. Pipe extra balls of meringue at the ends of each finger to make the bone shapes.
4 Bake for 1¼-1½ hours until crisp. Leave to cool on the paper.

Meringue pumpkins

Make as recipe above but pipe 7.5cm/3in diameter pumpkin shapes on to the paper. Thinly slice plain liquorice sweets and cut into triangles. Position for eyes. Cut short lengths of liquorice 'bootlaces' and use to shape mouths. Add stalks of thick green or black liquorice. Bake as above.

Witch's hat biscuit

Makes one hat

280g/10oz plain flour
55g/2oz cocoa powder
175g/6oz unsalted butter, softened
  and cubed
175g/6oz dark muscovado sugar
1 tbsp black treacle
2 eggs, beaten
55g/2oz plain chocolate, melted
85g/3oz icing sugar, sifted
1 tbsp lightly beaten egg white

1 Process the flour, cocoa powder and butter until the mixture resembles breadcrumbs. (Or rub the butter into the flour, then add the cocoa.)
2 Add the sugar, treacle and eggs and mix to a dough. Chill for 30 minutes.
3 Preheat the oven to 190C/375F/Gas 5. Lightly grease two baking sheets. Roll out a third of the dough on a lightly floured surface and cut out a 20cm/8in round using a plate as a guide. Transfer to a baking sheet.
4 Roll out remaining dough and trim to a 30cm/12in square. Transfer to a baking sheet. Mark the square into four 30 x 7.5cm/12 x 3in rectangles. Cut diagonally across each to give eight triangles. (You need six for the hat.)
5 Use trimmings to make star and crescent shapes. Bake the biscuit dough for 12 minutes or until beginning to colour around the edges.
6 While still warm, cut through the marked lines to separate the triangles. Cool on a wire rack.
7 Cool the melted chocolate until it begins to thicken. Spread a little down the straight sides and base of two of the triangles. Position over the round biscuit base so that the long sides touch. Spread more chocolate down the sides and bases of four of the remaining biscuit sections and secure. (Slip a large round biscuit cutter over the top to support it until the chocolate sets.)
8 Whisk together the icing sugar and egg white to a piping consistency, then use to outline star and crescent shapes. Leave to dry before securing to biscuit with melted chocolate.

Christmas is a great time to throw a party but with so many other things to organize and do, it's easy to run out of time and energy and either give up on the party or simply buy peanuts and plonk. If you start by thinking ahead, you can forget all that and try some of these delicious party ideas. All of the canapés can be made and frozen weeks before the party and will serve a drinks party of 20. We also include a recipe for party punch. So get cracking and planning and start inviting your guests.

christmas
party

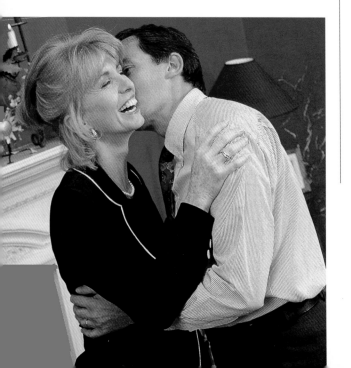

Turkey and sausage roulades

These have a lovely festive flavour and can be served warm or cold. Chicken fillets can be used instead of turkey.

Makes 60

4 large skinless turkey breast fillets
225g/8oz herby pork sausagemeat
25g/1oz pistachio nuts
1 tbsp chopped fresh parsley
40g/1½ oz cranberries, thawed if frozen
16 rashers rindless streaky bacon, stretched
salt and freshly ground black pepper
black grapes and vine leaves, to serve

1 Preheat the oven to 190C/375F/Gas 5. Flatten the turkey fillets by covering with a sheet of plastic film and beating with a rolling pin.
2 Mix the sausagemeat with the pistachios, parsley and seasoning, then divide into four and press evenly on top of each flattened turkey fillet. Arrange cranberries, end to end along the long side, then roll up the fillet from the longest side like a Swiss roll.
3 Tightly wind four rashers of bacon round each turkey roll, overlapping the bacon slightly as you wind, to completely enclose. Roast for 20 minutes or until cooked through. Cool slightly before cutting into slices, or cool completely. Arrange on platters with the grapes and the vine leaves.

FREEZING TIP Before cooking, cover the roulades in plastic film, then foil and freeze. Use within 2 months. To serve from the freezer: thaw in the fridge, unwrap, then roast as above.

Thai spiced fish cakes

Although ideal served warm, these are just as tasty once cooled.

Makes 60

900g/2lb skinless boneless cod fillets, thawed
*   if frozen*
2 red chillies, seeded and finely chopped
2 lemon grass stalks, very finely chopped
8 tbsp chopped fresh coriander
2 garlic cloves, crushed
2 tsp sugar
2 tsp salt
2 eggs
2 tbsp cornflour
3-6 tbsp sunflower oil, for frying
2 x 190ml bottles Thai chilli dipping sauce,
*   to serve*

1 Finely chop the cod in a food processor, then add remaining ingredients. Process again until very well blended.
2 Take teaspoons of the mixture and, using your hands, shape roughly into small fish cakes – you should end up with about 60.
3 Heat the oil in a large non-stick frying pan and fry the fish cakes, in batches, for two minutes each side or until golden. Serve with dipping sauce.

> **FREEZING TIP** Once cooked, cool the Fish cakes quickly and pack into a rigid container, interleaving the layers with freezer film. Use within 1 month. To serve from the freezer: thaw completely, then arrange on lightly greased baking sheets. Warm in an oven preheated to 200C/400F/Gas 6 for 8-10 minutes or until piping hot, then serve with dipping sauce.

Smoked salmon spirals

If you are not a fan of goat's cheese, use cream cheese instead.

Makes 50

400g pkt salmon slices
3 x 150g tubs mild soft goat's cheese
1-2 tbsp creamed horseradish
2 tbsp snipped fresh chives
2 tsp chopped fresh dill (optional), plus fresh
*   sprigs, to garnish*
freshly ground black pepper

1 Separate the salmon slices into strips, lay out, overlapping slightly, to make two long rectangles.
2 Beat together the goat's cheese, horseradish, herbs and pepper, then spread over the salmon.
3 Roll up tightly from the longest side to make two Swiss rolls, wrap in plastic film and chill before slicing. Serve garnished with fresh dill.

> **FREEZING TIP** Wrap the spirals in plastic film and foil, freeze on fast freeze setting until solid. Use within 1 month. To serve from the freezer: thaw in the fridge, slice and garnish.

Gruyère and chutney bite-size croissants

These are scrumptious and are made using ready-to-bake croissant dough, available in the chilled section of most large supermarkets.

Each flavour makes 36

240g can ready-to-bake croissant dough
mango chutney
200g/7oz Gruyère, cut into 36 mini rectangles,
* plus grated Gruyère, for sprinkling*
beaten egg, to glaze
fresh herbs, to garnish (optional)

1 Preheat the oven to 200C/400F/Gas 6. Unravel the croissant dough and cut through the perforations to make six pieces. Cut each piece, as evenly as possible, into six triangles.
2 Spread the dough with the mango chutney, place a piece of cheese at the longest side of each triangle and tightly roll up. Curve the ends to make the classic croissant shape.
3 Arrange on lightly greased baking sheets, then brush with beaten egg and scatter with grated cheese. Bake for 8-10 minutes or until golden. Serve garnished with fresh herbs, if using.

VARIATIONS

• **Pâté and cranberry croissants**
Make as previous recipe replacing the cheese with 200g/7oz pork liver pâté and the mango chutney with cranberry sauce.
• **Sausage and mustard croissants**
Make as above, replacing the cheese with 36 part-cooked cocktail sausages and the chutney with made English mustard. Sprinkle with poppy seeds before baking.

FREEZING TIP Once cooked, cool the croissants quickly, then pack into rigid containers, interleaving with layers of freezer film. Or, freeze before baking. Use within 2 months.
To serve from the freezer: thaw, reheat in an oven preheated to 200C/400F/Gas 6 for 5-6 minutes until heated through, then garnish.

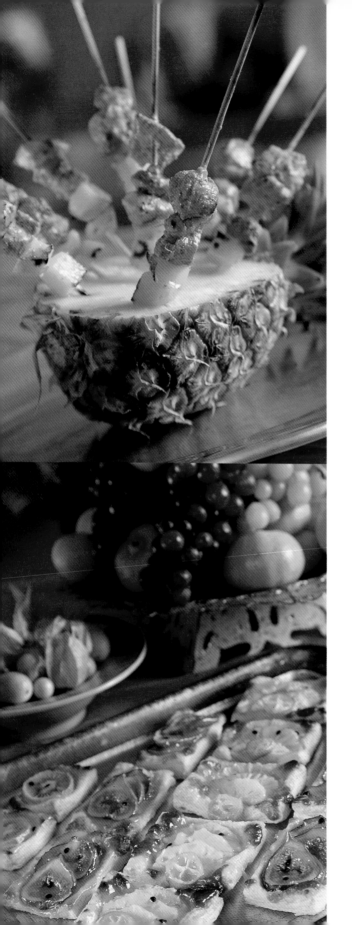

Ginger spiced pork with coconut

To save a last-minute panic, grill these in advance, then gently warm through in the oven, covered with foil, once your guests have arrived.

Makes 40

200ml carton coconut cream
2-3 tbsp Rogan Josh curry paste
2 tbsp grated fresh root ginger
900g/2lb pork steaks, cubed
2 mangoes, peeled, stoned and cubed
juice and grated rind of 1 lime
salt and freshly ground black pepper
1 fresh pineapple, halved, to serve (optional)

1 Mix together the coconut cream, curry paste, ginger and seasoning, then stir in the pork and marinate for 1 hour.
2 Mix the mangoes with the lime juice and rind, then thread on to satay sticks with the pork. Grill for 8 minutes or until the pork is cooked and beginning to go golden. Serve while still warm speared into the pineapple halves, if using, or arranged on a platter.

> **FREEZING TIP** Cover and freeze the marinated pork before cooking and use within 1 month. To serve from the freezer: thaw the pork and marinade in the fridge, then continue from step 2.

Ginger spiced pork with coconut (top)
Kiwi fruit and marzipan pastries (below)

Kiwi fruit and marzipan pastries

The number of pastries you get per pastry sheet depends on the fruit that you choose. Ideally go for a selection of three varieties.

Makes 32

375g puff pastry sheet, thawed if frozen
85g/3oz marzipan
8 large kiwi fruit
5 tbsp apricot jam
sieved pulp of 2 passion fruit, plus a few seeds

1 Preheat the oven to 220C/425F/Gas 7. Unravel the pastry, then grate the marzipan evenly over the surface.
2 Peel, then trim the ends from the kiwi fruit and cut into even slices, about four per fruit depending on the size. Arrange evenly spaced on the pastry, four slices down and eight slices along, then, using a sharp knife, cut the pastry between the fruit slices so you end up with neat oblongs with slices of kiwi on top.
3 Place on wetted baking sheets and cook for 10-12 minutes or until the pastry is cooked. Mix the jam and the passion fruit and brush generously over the pastries to glaze

- **Pineapple and kumquat pastries**
Make as above replacing the kiwi fruit with three thin slices of fresh pineapple and a slice of kumquat per pastry square.
- **Fresh fig pastries**
Make as above, replacing the kiwi fruit with two slices of fig per pastry square.

> **FREEZING TIP** Once cool, pack the pastries into rigid containers before glazing, interleaving with freezer film. Use within 1 month.
> To serve from the freezer: refresh in an oven preheated to 220C/425F/Gas 7 for a few minutes to recrisp the pastry. Glaze and serve.

Sparkling fruit punch

To make this fruit punch more alcoholic, replace the grape juice with a bottle of chilled sparkling white wine.

Makes 10 long drinks

50ml/2fl oz Pernod
1 litre/1³/4 pints tropical fruit drink or pink grapefruit juice
1/2 red grapefruit, segmented
1 lemon, halved and thinly sliced
1/2 star fruit, sliced
1 litre/1³/4 pints sparkling white grape juice
fresh lemon geranium or mint leaves

1 Pour the Pernod into a large jug or punch bowl, then add the fruit juice and fruit. Just before serving, add the grape juice, geranium or mint leaves and plenty of ice.

decorating with flowers

T here is nothing like a bunch of flowers to cheer you up and nowadays there are all sorts of ways to display them without having to be good at those tricky formal arrangements. This chapter has some beautiful ideas and some of them are amazingly simple and effective; all of them will help to make your home look prettier and more welcoming without taking too much time and trouble.

How often have you been given a bunch of flowers and not known how to make the best of them? Well, here are some great ideas to make the most of your blooms whether they are shop bought or picked from the garden. Copy these displays, or adapt them to make them your own. For example instead of oranges use pumpkins or melons as vases, simply lining with a plastic bag to make them waterproof. Our strawberry punch idea can also be adapted by displaying almost anything around the flowers.

unusual *flower* pots

Moss pot

YOU WILL NEED

vase or old goldfish bowl • **moss** • PVA adhesive • **mangetout** • 'Ambience' roses • **veronica**

Cover the vase or goldfish bowl with glue, then cover completely with moss, pressing it lightly into place. Cut mangetout halfway down the middle so that they resemble old-fashioned pegs, and 'peg' around the top of the jar. Tie the flowers into a bunch and insert into the bowl with water. Hide the stems by tucking extra moss around the top of the bowl.

Shaker style

YOU WILL NEED

sugar shaker • **poppies**

Partly fill a sugar shaker with water. Choose delicately coloured poppies with naturally curved stems and push them through the holes at the top of the shaker.

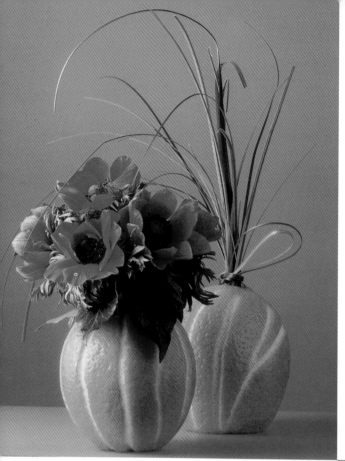

Citrus cups

YOU WILL NEED

zester or canelle knife · **oranges** · apple corer · **anemones** · bear grass · **plastic test tubes or bags**

Using a zester or canelle knife, make a pattern on the orange rinds. Hollow out the centres with an apple corer and trim the bases so they sit flat. Place the flowers or bear grass in the test tubes or bags filled with water and sit in the orange. Trim the tops of the plastic bags as and where necessary.

Fruit punch

YOU WILL NEED

red anemones · **roses** · string · **glass tumbler** · goldfish bowl · vase · **strawberries** · sparkling white wine

Loosely tie the flowers together with string. Cut stems to the same length and place in a glass tumbler with water. Sit the tumbler inside the goldfish bowl vase. Fill the vase with strawberries and sparkling wine.

Teapot treat

YOU WILL NEED

red and pink roses • **red arum lilies** • purple
prairie-gentian • **blue anemone** • lilac •
red gerbera • string • **plain teapot**

Tie the flowers together in a bunch
with string, cut the stems to the same
length and place in a plain teapot
with water.

Line dance

YOU WILL NEED

rectangular glass vase • **cartons of mustard and cress** • Parrot tulips

Remove the mustard and cress from their cartons and
arrange in the base of the vase. Add water, then push the
tulip stems down into the cress to hold in place (the cress
will be inedible).

Fancy fry-up (*not illustrated*)

YOU WILL NEED

frying pan • **5cm high piece fresh flower florist's foam** • florist's tape
• **sweetcorn cobs with husks** • fresh rosemary sprigs • **marigolds**

Cut the foam to fit the frying pan. Remove from the pan
and immerse in water to saturate, then secure to the pan
with florist's tape. Push the sweetcorn cobs into the foam.
Cover the foam with rosemary sprigs, then add the
marigolds at varying heights.

Flower rings or wreaths are one of the prettiest ways of decorating your home at any time of the year. I always hang one on my front door at Christmas, made with evergreen and berried leaves bought from my local greengrocer and mixed with foliage from the garden. This year, I plan to make the Frosted rose wreath, (page 116), to welcome my guests. All the materials you need for the Hop ring and the Frosted rose wreath should be available at your florist, but it's a good idea to order in advance.

door
wreaths

Hop ring

YOU WILL NEED

hops, enough to tie into 9 bunches and stems trimmed to 7.5cm long • **rosemary, enough to tie into 9 bunches and stems trimmed to 7.5cm long** • florist's wire • **25 dried red roses, stems trimmed to 7.5cm long** • 15 dried orange slices • **30 dried red and green apple slices** • 15 dried sweet potato slices • **35cm diameter twig ring** • ball of twine

1 Preparing the hops, rosemary and roses Tie the hops and rosemary separately into nine generous bunches using the florist's wire. Tie the roses into five bunches of five flower heads.

2 Preparing the dried fruits Tie about 15 bunches of three, four or five fruit slices using the florist's wire. Twist the wire ends together to leave a 7.5cm tail to each of the bunches.

3 Covering the ring Tie the end of the twine to the twig wreath and attach the bunches of fruits, flowers, hops and herbs by winding the twine over their stems. Add the bunches in a regular order and in a herringbone pattern so they completely cover the twig base. Tuck the stems of the last bunches under the heads of the first. Secure and trim the twine.

Frosted rose wreath

YOU WILL NEED

35cm diameter fresh flower florist's foam ring • **snowberry stems, variegated holly, rosemary** • 30 stems cream roses, stems trimmed to 7.5cm long • **59 stems dark red cosmos, stems trimmed to 7.5cm long** • 3 bunches green grapes • **caster sugar** • egg whites • **florist's wire** • 1m blue and 2m apricot ribbon (both 5cm wide) • **3 clematis seed heads** • gold spray paint

1 Preparing the ring Immerse the foam ring in water for about 20 minutes to saturate and sort the foliage and flowers.

2 Creating a foliage outline Set the size and style of the wreath by pushing short stems of rosemary, holly and snowberry into the ring. Everything added after the foliage will be placed within this basic framework.

3 Adding the fruit Add three bunches of frosted grapes (to make, brush the grapes with beaten egg white, then dust with caster sugar) to the wreath by laying them on the ring and securing firmly with wire.

4 Adding the flowers and the ribbon Add the roses around the wreath in groups of three, then intersperse the roses with bunches of cosmos. Tie the blue ribbon into a bow and attach a wire to the back to form a short stem. Position the bow at the top of the wreath and secure with the wire. Weave the apricot ribbon between the flowers around the wreath, securing to the foam ring with short hairpin-shaped wires.

5 Finishing touches Dust the clematis seed heads with gold spray paint and group together around the centre of the bow, pushing the stems into the foam. Lightly spray whole wreath with gold paint.

It's much more exciting to receive a hand-tied bunch of flowers like this than to get them layered in a long bag which then needs to be sorted and arranged. With a hand-tied bouquet the bunch is ready to put straight into a vase, looking perfect. I always thought they would be really tricky to do but, in fact, with a little practice it's much easier than it looks.

hand-tied
bouquet

Hand-tied bouquet

The aim is to make this arrangement in your hand, evenly distributing the flowers and foliage throughout the bouquet. While building this arrangement, the stems are spiralled so that the point at which they cross is narrow. This is particularly useful, as a large number of flowers can fit neatly through the narrow neck of a bulbous-shaped vase, which will hold them in place when the binding is cut.

YOU WILL NEED

30 stems montbretia · **20 stems yellow roses** · 10 stems purple lizianthus · **10 stems cotinus foliage** · 10 stems kniphofia (Red hot pokers) · **string** · raffia or ribbon (optional) · **vase (ours was 25cm high)**

Preparing the flowers and foliage Open up the bunches and separate out the stems cutting them all to a similar and manageable length. Remove the leaves and any thorns from the lower half of the stems. Be careful not to cut them too short as it is better to trim the stems to fit the container when you have finished the arrangement than to cut them too short. For ease of assembly, keep the different flowers and foliage in separate piles.

1 Beginning the spiralling Take a fairly sturdy piece of foliage and hold it loosely, between the base of your thumb and forefinger, approximately two-thirds down the stem from the top of the flower head. Add a second flower at a slight angle to the first stem. Then turn the stems in your hand a little before adding another stem. See Tip for further details.

2 Adding more stems Continue adding stems in this way. Always angle them in the same direction and turn the whole bunch a few degrees each time you add a new stem. Work through the different flowers and foliage in repeating sequence until all the materials are used. This ensures that the different elements are distributed evenly throughout the arrangement.

3 Binding the bouquet Without losing your grip on the arrangement, tie the stems firmly with string around the point where the stems cross.

4 Trimming the stems Cut the stems so that they extend below the binding point by about one-third of the overall height of the display. As long as the binding point is secure, and the display well balanced, a sharp tap of the cut stems on the table top will enable the arrangement to stand on its own.

5 Adding the finishing touch

If you are presenting the bouquet as a gift, add a decorative flourish with raffia, or a co-ordinating coloured ribbon, tied around the binding point. Otherwise place the flowers in a vase. If a slightly looser effect is required, cut the string when the arrangement is in position.

TIP

If you are right-handed, hold the flowers in your left hand, add the stems at an angle of 11 and 5 o'clock, and turn the bunch anti-clockwise, away from you.

Left-handed people should hold the flowers in their right hand, add stems at an angle of 1 and 7 o'clock and turn the bunch clockwise, away from them.

The great advantage of dried flower arrangements is that they last, not forever, but for at least a year and the sculptured style of these arrangements tend to maintain their looks and shape longer than most. Topiary flower trees are surprisingly easy to make, though they do take several hours to do, so choose a day when you are feeling patient. We bought the flowers for these designs, but it is well worth drying your own. Fresh rosebuds are a good investment, since you can enjoy them in a fresh arrangement first, then dry them.

dried *flower* topiary

To dry successfully, loosely tie the flowers in small bunches and hang them upside down in a warm room. Even droopy headed blooms will dry straight.

Miniature pink topiary tree

This display of tiny pink rosebuds is made in a similar way to the larger yellow topiary tree (page 124). However, the scale is smaller and because we used only one flower type, this arrangement is much quicker, cheaper and simpler to make.

YOU WILL NEED

suitable container (ours was 10cm sq x 12.5cm high) • **plastic sheet** • 'dry hard' clay • **5 x 25cm long cinnamon sticks (available from florists)** • string • **10cm diameter dried flower foam ball** • all-purpose glue, such as Uhu (optional) • **2 bunches lavender, stems trimmed to 7.5cm long** • 5 x 20 head bunches tiny dried pink rosebuds, stems trimmed to 5cm long

1 **Preparing the container** Line the container with protective plastic sheet and fill with 'dry hard' clay to 2.5cm below the rim.

2 **Making the trunk** Tie the cinnamon sticks together with string to form a single trunk, then snip with scissors to a length in proportion to your pot and flower ball. Push the trunk into the centre of the clay, and push the foam ball on top of the trunk. Secure with glue, if you feel this is necessary.

3 **Decorating the pot** Trim the plastic sheet level with the surface of the clay. Working with bunches of five lavender stems, push them into the clay surface until the clay is obscured. Try to keep the lavender flowers at the same height. Trim when complete to achieve an attractively neat even surface.

4 **Decorating the ball** Push the rosebud stems, one at a time, into the foam ball as close together as possible.

Yellow rose tree

At a glance you may well think this yellow rose tree is an extravagant arrangement until you appreciate its size – it stands over 70cm high. If you choose to make a smaller one, keep the size of the pot, the ball and the height of the trunk in proportion with each other. Remember, too, that when the ball is covered with flowers and foliage it will increase its size by several inches.

YOU WILL NEED

suitable container (ours was 25cm sq x 17.5cm high) · **plastic sheet** · 'dry hard' clay or plaster of Paris · **10 birch twigs** · string · **15cm diameter dried flower foam ball** · all-purpose glue such as Uhu (optional) · **moss, to cover the pot surface** · florist's wire · **10 stems preserved eucalyptus, stems trimmed to 7.5cm long** · 2 bunches wheat, stems trimmed to 7.5cm long · **30 stems dried achillea, stems trimmed to 7.5cm long** · 6 x 20 head bunches dried yellow roses, stems trimmed to 7.5cm long

1 Preparing the container
Line the container with protective plastic sheet and fill with 'dry hard' clay or plaster of Paris to 2.5cm below the rim.

2 Making the trunk Bunch together the birch twigs and tie the stems firmly with string at two points about 30cm apart. Trim the stems 2.5cm beyond the tied points at either end, to form a 35cm long trunk. Push one end of the twig trunk firmly into the centre of the clay in the pot.

3 **Adding the foam ball** Push the foam ball down on top of the twig trunk. If necessary, add glue to secure. Trim the plastic sheet level with the surface of the clay, then cover with moss securing it with hairpin-shaped wires.

4 **Creating the foliage outline** Push in the eucalyptus stems, randomly but evenly, over the entire surface of the foam ball to create an outline. Add the wheat in the same way.

5 **Adding the achillea** Push the achillea stems evenly into the foam, distributing them among the wheat and eucalyptus.

6 **Adding the roses** Push the rose stems into the foam ball in groups of three, ensuring they are distributed evenly and fill in any remaining gaps.

Candlesticks make perfect stands for flower arrangements. They give them extra height and grandeur and you don't need to use nearly as many flowers as you would in a vase. Don't feel you can only use these displays in the evening – they look just as good in daylight, although obviously they really come into their own after dark. The easiest way to make these displays is to buy specially designed candle cups that slot into the candlesticks.

WARNING The utmost care must be taken when the candles are lit, that they do not burn right down into the foliage.

candlestick *flower* arrangements

Fruits and bay

FOR EACH ARRANGEMENT YOU WILL NEED

1 block fresh flower florist's foam • **black plastic candle cup or bowl** • 1 candlestick • **gold candle** • narrow florist's tape • **6 stems bay leaves** • 30cm long 22 gauge stub wires • **3 small bunches green grapes** • 20 lychees • **2 small nectarines or apricots** • 20 cherries

1 Using saturated fresh flower foam, prepare and attach candle cup, foam and candles (page 128).

2 Trim the bay into short stems and push into the foam around the candle to create a foliage outline for the display.

3 Trim the wires and bend to form long hairpin shapes; these are used to secure the fruit to the foam. Start by fixing the bunches of grapes to the foam so that they hang down the candlestick below the arrangement. Add the lychees one at a time, grouping them in threes, then add the nectarines and cherries.

Winter snow

The effect of white and green flowers and foliage displayed against this classical bust is quite breathtaking.

YOU WILL NEED

silver candle cup or bowl · **1 block fresh flower florist's foam** · three branch candelabra · **Blu-tac (optional)** · narrow florist's tape · **3 tall green candles** · ivy stem · **rosemary and snowberry foliage** · 10 stems white spray roses · **6 stems white lizianthus** · euphorbia

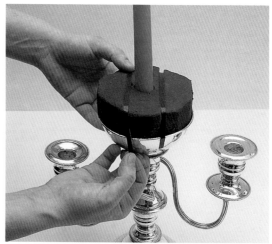

1 Preparing the candelabra For this display, soak the foam in water to saturate, then trim to fit inside the candle cup. It should stand 3-4 cm above the bowl rim. Push a candle down into the centre of the foam. Slot the candle cup into the central hole of the candelabra; you may need to use a little Blu-tac to hold it firm. Secure the foam in the bowl with the florist's tape, then slot in the remaining candles.

2 Creating the foliage outline Wrap a stem of ivy around the branches of the candelabra, then define the size of your display by creating a foliage outline using the stems of rosemary. It can be small and tight, or loose and flowing similar to this one. Add several foliage stems of snowberry to the display outline before arranging the flowers loosely within the boundaries of the foliage.

3 Adding the flowers Trim the small stems off the spray roses and arrange each stem individually in the foam to create an open effect. Add the lizianthus among the roses. Use more open blooms towards the centre of the display. Add euphorbia to soften the overall appearance.

Citrus slice

Both branches of this candlestick are decorated with a compact arrangement of dried flowers. If the arrangement is to be displayed in front of a mirror, take care that it looks good from all angles.

YOU WILL NEED

2 black plastic candle cups · **dried flower florist's foam, dry** · two branch candelabra · **narrow florist's tape** · 2 blue candles · **10 stems dried eucalyptus, stems trimmed to 7.5cm long** · 1 bunch dried ornamental grass, stems trimmed to 7.5cm long · **22 gauge florist's wire** · 60 dried orange slices · **1 bunch dried lavender, stems trimmed to 7.5cm long** · 30 stems dried red roses, stems trimmed to 7.5cm long · **gold spray paint (optional)**

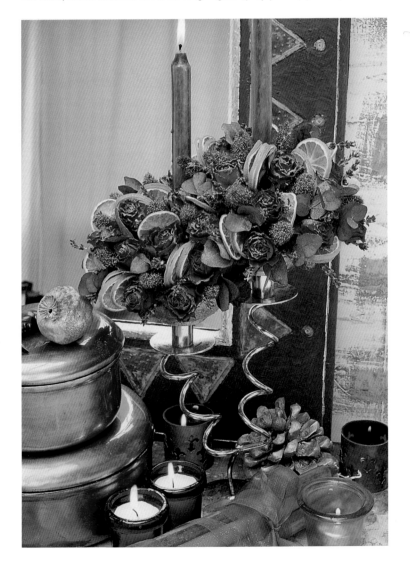

TIP

Specially designed candle cups, that slot into candlesticks, come in white, black and silver coloured plastic and are available from florists. They can also be spray painted to complement your display. Alternatively, you can neatly, but securely, tape a small bowl in place. It is just as effective.

1 Prepare and attach candle cups, dry foam and candles.

2 Push individual eucalyptus and ornamental grass stems into the foam around the candles to build up a foliage outline for the display.

3 Using the wire, tie the orange slices together in groups of three, leaving a 7.5cm long tail. Add the orange slices to the arrangement spacing them evenly and prettily among the foliage.

4 Add the lavender and rose stems evenly to the arrangement. A dusting of gold paint provides the finishing touch.

Here are three super ideas to help you decorate your home for a party during the winter and especially at Christmas. The Fruit pyramid is the most ambitious but equally the most impressive, while the Candelabra ring is very pretty. But it's the mirrored candle display that is my favourite because it costs little and you can make it in five minutes. Do remember to be careful with these winter displays: candles and berries look wonderful but can be hazardous, so take great care and keep them out of the reach of children.

winter *warming* displays

Fruit pyramid

This arrangement makes a stunning table centre but it will only stay fresh for a day. The spiralling fruits are secured to the cone with cocktail sticks.

YOU WILL NEED

1 large or 3 small blocks dried flower florist's foam • **florist's tape** • 1 pineapple top • **35 x 15cm piece chicken wire** • stand or dish • **76 cocktail sticks** • 22 small satsumas • **24 greengages** • 8 kiwi fruit, cut in half • **14 Chinese gooseberries** • ivy leaves

1 **Preparing the base** Carve a cone shape, 20cm high with a 12cm diameter base, from the large piece of foam. If you are using three blocks stacked together, secure together with tape before shaping. Slice 5cm from the top of the cone and replace with the pineapple top. Wrap the chicken wire around the cone and trim to fit. Bend the ends together to join, then tuck the edges under the cone, and over the pineapple.

2 **Adding the fruit** Place the cone on a stand or suitable dish. The fruits are added in spiralling bands, each fruit being held in place with a cocktail stick initially skewered into the back of the fruit, then pushed into the cone at an angle. To create the foundation for the design, attach a spiralling ring of satsumas to the cone (picture below), then fill in with greengages, below and kiwi fruit, above. Continue with more satsumas and greengages and finish with a ring of Chinese gooseberries around the top.

3 **Adding the finishing touch** Any gaps in the display can be covered with ivy leaves. These can be pushed between the fruits and held in place by the chicken wire.

Candelabra ring

This very pretty table display will last for several days provided you keep the foam ring moist and replace the candles. Be sure to protect the table surface from candle wax and water.

YOU WILL NEED

40cm fresh flower florist's foam ring · **2 bunches guelder rose foliage with berries, stems trimmed to 7.5cm long** · 6 limes · **3 x 5cm long florist's stub wires, plus extra for the ivy (optional)** · 1 bunch ivy leaf trails · **candelabra** · 10 stems dark blue lizianthus · **9 stems small reddish green anthurium** · 9 stems red gerbera

1 Preparing the ring Soak the foam ring in water until saturated. Create the outline of the arrangement using the guelder rose foliage. Push the stems into the foam to evenly cover the ring surface.

2 Adding the fruit The limes are displayed in pairs. Skewer the back of each lime with wire, then push the wires into the ring to secure in place.

3 Decorating the candelabra Entwine the ivy trails around the branches of the candelabra, using wire to secure the ivy in place, if needed. Place the foam ring on the table where it is going to be displayed and position the candelabra in the centre. Embed its feet in the foam ring to keep it stable, if necessary.

4 Adding the flowers Trim the the lizianthus, anthurium and gerbera flower stems to a suitable length, about 8-10cm, and add them to the ring in attractive groups of two or three, filling any gaps. Add the candles.

Candle-lit tray

This is a very quick and easy arrangement that can be made from bits and pieces around your home and garden. If you don't have a spare mirror or silver tray, cover a plain tray or chopping board with foil – the effect is almost as good. Another good tip, is to buy a few tall candles, then cut them down to various heights.

YOU WILL NEED

ornamental mirror, or silver tray • **6 x 5cm diameter candles of various heights** • garden foliage (we used yew, ivy and snowberries)

1 Group the candles at one end of the mirror or tray and arrange the foliage around the edge allowing the candle light to reflect in the surface.

Herbs have a knack of always looking beautiful, whether they are growing in your garden, sprouting from a pot, or hanging dried from the rafters in your kitchen. One of the most attractive ways of using them is to make herb wreaths. These can be made using either fresh or dried material.

The advantage of using fresh, is that the herbs are more flexible and easy to use; the disadvantage is that you can't always be sure how they will dry. Try to pick your herbs early when the dew has dried, but before the sun has drawn out their volatile oils.

aromatic *herbs*

To dry, strip off any spoiled leaves, and leave the stems long. Gather into scanty bunches, then hang upside-down in a warm place. Sage, thyme, bay leaves, marjoram and oregano dry the most attractively. Other ideas for using herbs include flavoured oils and vinegars and pretty, yet practical bouquets garnis.

Garden herb wreath

YOU WILL NEED

22 gauge florist's wire • **fresh herbs (we used sage, thyme, bay leaves, dill, rosemary, flatleaf parsley, basil and chives)** • carrot tops • **lavender** • ball of twine • **35cm diameter twig ring** • 2 small Victorian 'long tom' garden pots • **24 cinnamon sticks** • raffia • **bag of bun moss** • floral adhesive (optional)

1 Preparing the herbs Using the wire, tie the fresh herbs, carrot tops and lavender into generous bunches. Trim the stems to about 7.5cm close to the ties. You will need about 30 bunches.

2 Attaching the herbs Tie the end of the twine to the 'top' of the twig wreath and attach the bunches of carrot tops, lavender and herbs, in a regular order and in a herringbone pattern, by winding the twine over their stems to entirely cover three-quarters of the right-hand side. Secure and trim the twine. Repeat to cover the left side of the ring in the same way, leaving a space at the base for the pots.

3 Adding the pots Attach wires to the pots, then tie firmly on to the base of the wreath. Fill the pots with fresh herbs.

4 Add the cinnamon stick bundles Using the wire, tie the cinnamon into four bundles of six sticks, twisting the wire ends together to leave a 15cm tail to each bunch. Tie raffia around the bundles to cover the wire. Attach the cinnamon sticks to the wreath by pushing the wires through to the back and securing. Finish by covering any gaps with bun moss, held in place with floral adhesive or wire.

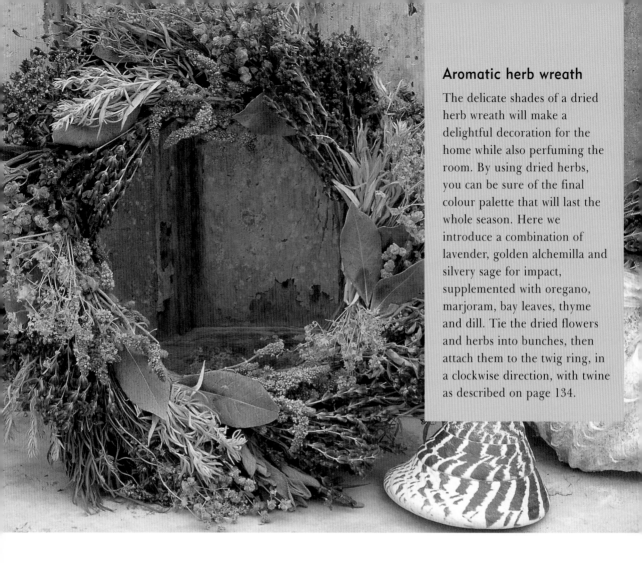

Aromatic herb wreath

The delicate shades of a dried herb wreath will make a delightful decoration for the home while also perfuming the room. By using dried herbs, you can be sure of the final colour palette that will last the whole season. Here we introduce a combination of lavender, golden alchemilla and silvery sage for impact, supplemented with oregano, marjoram, bay leaves, thyme and dill. Tie the dried flowers and herbs into bunches, then attach them to the twig ring, in a clockwise direction, with twine as described on page 134.

Bouquets garnis

Originally, bouquets garnis (sometimes called faggots of herbs) were simply tiny bundles of herbs tied with string and used for flavouring soups and stews. They can be made up with fresh herbs, tied with thread, and hung up in garlands, to be snipped off when needed. Or, the herbs can be dried, then tied in little squares of muslin and stored until needed. Whichever type of bouquets garnis you choose to make, don't forget to remove it before serving the finished dish.

Traditionally, bouquets garnis were made up with a blade of mace or a couple of cloves, a few peppercorns, a crumbled bay leaf, parsley, rosemary and thyme sprigs, wrapped in muslin.

You may like to try experimenting with alternative herb combinations for particular dishes. The following are some of the more popular mixes:

For beef and lamb, try sage, rosemary and bay leaf.
For chicken dishes, try tarragon, thyme and marjoram.
For fish dishes, try dill, tarragon and lemon balm.

Herb oils and vinegars

Aromatic oils and vinegars take their flavours from newly cut herbs, but make sure there's no trace of dampness or damage or they could take on a musty flavour. You can create your own flavour combinations or follow our recipes below.

YOU WILL NEED

Airtight bottles that are well washed, rinsed, and dried in a warm oven to sterilize. Use plastic screw tops or corks to seal, avoid metal tops for vinegars • Oil with a delicate flavour, such as sunflower or rape seed, is best for lightly flavoured and pale oils. For a more Mediterranean flavour, use a good quality virgin olive oil.

Method Pour the oil into a wide-necked jar and add your chosen herbs and spices, pushing them below the surface of the oil. Cover and leave for one week, shaking the jar each day. Strain into clean bottles and discard flavouring. Add a few herbs or peppercorns for decoration. Seal tightly and store in a cool place out of direct sunlight.

Mediterranean oil To 500ml/18fl oz sunflower oil, add 8 bay leaves, 8 thyme sprigs, 12 roughly broken dried red chillies, 8 halved garlic cloves and 12 roughly crushed peppercorns. This is delicious brushed over grilled and barbecued meat, poultry and fish.

Olive oil with basil To 500ml/18fl oz extra virgin olive oil, add 50g/1¾ oz roughly chopped fresh basil leaves and 12 roughly crushed peppercorns. This oil is ideal for drizzling over tomato and mozzarella salads, grilled tomatoes and for marinating fish.

Mixed herb oil Mix 300ml/½ pint olive oil and 300ml/½ pint sunflower oil with 75g/2¾ oz mixed fresh herbs such as sage, thyme, tarragon, marjoram, oregano and lemon balm.

Spiced orange and rosemary vinegar To 700ml/1¼ pints red wine vinegar, add the thinly pared rind from an unwaxed orange (use a potato peeler and cut as thinly as possible to avoid the pith), 8 rosemary sprigs, two teaspoons crushed juniper berries and half a teaspoon crushed black peppercorns.

Cider vinegar with mint and coriander
To 700ml/1¼ pints cider vinegar, add 50g/1¾ oz torn mint leaves, six tea-spoons roughly crushed coriander seeds and half a teaspoon crushed black peppercorns. This is particularly delicious over cucumber, or mix with oil and use as a dressing for melon, tomatoes and prawns.

Topiary is becoming an increasingly popular form of garden decoration and it's easy to see why. Shapes made out of evergreen plants bring stylish, living sculpture into your garden and, unlike seasonal flowers, topiaries maintain their splendour all year round.

There are two quite different methods of making these potted sculptures depending on whether you want an instant effect, as I do, or whether you have time to grow them slowly and properly. The cheat's way is to train climbing plants over a wire

potted
topiary

frame (ivy is especially good for this). The traditional way, of course, is by cutting and shaping small-leaved evergreen shrubs into recognizable forms whether it is a bird, a ball or a pyramid.

Easy topiary

Fast growing and pliable, plain coloured small-leaved ivy is the perfect plant for instant topiary using a frame.

YOU WILL NEED

broken crockery or fine gravel • **flowerpot in proportion to the frame** • medium-size bag all-purpose potting compost • **1 large or 3 small trailing ivy plants** • topiary frame • **galvanized wire** • wire ties or garden twine

1 **Potting the ivy** Place broken crockery or fine gravel at the base of the pot for drainage, add the compost to 10cm below the top, then plant the ivy in the centre, topping off with more compost.

2 **Securing the frame** Place the frame over the top of the pot and peg it down into the soil with 15cm long hairpin-shaped lengths of galvanized wire.

3 **Attaching the ivy to the frame** Unravel the strands of ivy and spread them evenly around the pot. Wind them, one at a time, on to the frame and attach with wire ties or garden twine.

4 **Maintenance** Water and feed regularly with liquid fertilizer to ensure rapid growth. Tie new strands across any remaining gaps on the frame until it is completely covered. Snip off surplus strands to keep a crisp outline.

TIP

Box, also known as boxwood, is most usually used because it is so adaptable to making small, dense shapes. You can also use Chinese privet or the tiny-leaved Chinese honeysuckle, which doesn't look like honeysuckle at all, but makes a small, fast-growing and easily shaped bush.

Selecting the right container for potted topiary is essential, as it can affect its growth and appearance. Before you start planting, choose a pot to complement your subject: simple geometric shapes look good in terracotta clay pots decorated with swags or other designs. Metal containers, in traditional or modern designs, look striking when planted with fancy shapes; galvanized buckets have a crisp, modern look and are effective when planted with simple ball, spirals or lollipop shapes. The interiors of porous pots should be painted with a waterproofing sealant before planting to prevent moisture loss from the soil.

Making a topiary bird

You can buy ready-made topiary birds from garden centres, but it is more fun to grow your own. You can use a topiary frame, with a ready-made outline, or shape the plant freehand – the way traditional cottage gardeners have made their topiaries for centuries. Box plants are the most suitable, because they are so amenable to clipping and shaping. The main thing is not to worry about cutting in the wrong place; the worst that can happen is that you will have to wait a little longer for that bit to grow again. You soon gain speed and confidence by getting used to trimming the bird and enjoying watching its shape develop.

Growing a bird freehand

Choose one half of the plant to be the body and head, and the other half to fashion into a tail. Start by tying the branches down on to a couple of canes that have been firmly inserted in a V-shape in the pot. Then, all you do is imagine the ultimate shape you want the bird to be, and picture the final shape as you cut and tie. Trim the plant to shape once in late spring, and again in summer, then watch and wait. You should have a rough bird-shape within two years, and a splendid avian specimen after three to four years.

Using a bird frame

A very easy way of training a topiary bird is to grow a box plant through a ready-made topiary frame. As the plant grows, you simply tie young branches into the framework and trim off surplus stray growth in spring and summer. Continue training and clipping until the template is filled out. You can then cut away the wire frame carefully, and continue to trim by eye in future years.

TIP

Remember to water potted topiaries regularly throughout the year and apply a weak solution of liquid fertilizer regularly throughout the spring and summer. Pot-on into a larger container after two or three years.

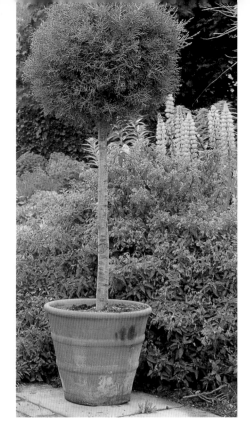

Lollipop tree

To make a standard, or 'lollipop' tree from scratch, start with a rooted cutting of box, bay, rosemary or cypress, as shown here, and allow the central (leader) stem to grow upwards. Tie the leader to a cane to encourage straight growth and pinch off side shoots, but retain leaves that are growing on the central stem itself. When it has achieved the desired height, pinch out the growing tip to encourage a bushing out of growth at the top. The rounded head will gradually develop as you pinch out the growing tips over a couple of years. Trim off the leaves on the main stalk so you have a clear stem. In future years you can trim with shears to maintain the ball shape at the top.

Cones

Cones make very stylish, formal topiary and are also the easiest of shapes to produce. You simply make a triangular template with three canes to provide the outline, and follow the direction of the sloping canes as you cut. Work around the bush, trimming off any branches that extend beyond the shape formed by the canes. Box, yew and bay are suitable plants for this treatment.

Topiary frames

These are available in many different shapes and sizes, and usually made from bent galvanised wire, or chicken wire. Bird shapes such as peacocks, chickens and ducks are popular but there are also spirals, lollipops and teddy bears. Suppliers include Avant Garden (0171-229 4408) and Wadham Trading Company (01367 850499).

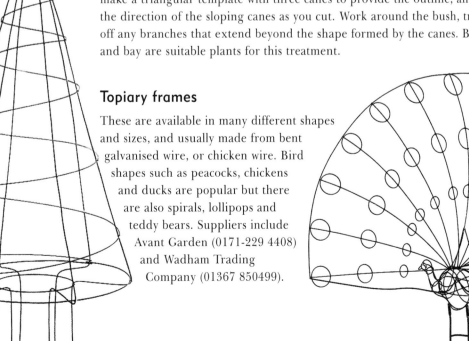

the big easy

Anyone who cooks every day for a family and says they never get bored is a better person than I am. What we all want nowadays, in our busy lives, are quick, easy but delicious and original ideas for producing economical everyday meals. Here are some of my favourites: I promise they'll go down well with the family and that you'll find them very little trouble to cook — you may even be surprised to find you're enjoying yourself, and that you have time to relax before the family descend.

Sweet chilli chicken

These finger-lickin' drumsticks taste absolutely
great. Eat hot, straight from the oven, or cold.
They can also be cooked on a barbecue.

Serves 6

12 meaty chicken drumsticks
2 garlic cloves, crushed
2 shallots, very finely chopped
6 tbsp clear honey
3 tbsp dark soy sauce
2 tbsp wholegrain mustard
1 tbsp Chinese chilli sauce

1 Place all the ingredients in a non-metallic dish
or rigid container and stir thoroughly until the
chicken is well coated.
2 Cover and marinate in the fridge for 4 hours
or preferably overnight, stirring a couple of times,
to ensure each drumstick gets a good soaking in
the sauce.
3 Preheat the oven to 200C/400F/Gas 6. Transfer
the chicken to a baking dish and roast for 35-40
minutes. Baste occasionally with the sauce to give
a sticky coating.

Preparation time: 5 minutes, plus marinating.
Cooking time: 40 minutes.
Calories per serving: 304.

THE BIG EASY

The recipes in this chapter are designed
for people who don't have much time to
cook, but who would still like to prepare
tasty, fast, healthy and economical meals
for their families.

Turkey chow mein

Fast and easy, fresh and light, full of vitamins
and eastern delight. For a vegetarian version,
substitute the turkey with Quorn.

Serves 2

250g/9oz egg thread noodles
3 tsp groundnut oil
1 onion, sliced
2 garlic cloves, crushed
2.5cm/1in fresh root ginger, finely chopped
450g/1lb turkey strips
1 red pepper, halved, seeded and cut into strips
225g/8oz mangetout, topped and tailed
small can baby sweetcorn, drained and halved
* lengthways or 100g pkt fresh baby sweetcorn,*
* halved*
2 tsp cornflour
1 tbsp sherry
2 tbsp dark soy sauce
2 tsp sesame oil

1 Place the noodles in a large jug and pour over
boiling water to cover. Stir with a fork and leave
to soak for 3 minutes, then strain.
2 Meanwhile, heat the oil in a wok or large frying
pan, add the onion and stir fry until translucent.
Add the garlic and ginger and continue stirring.
Toss in the turkey strips and stir fry for 2 minutes
or until the meat is sealed all over. Add the red
pepper, mangetout, baby corn and then stir fry
for 2 minutes.
3 In a small bowl, mix together the cornflour,
sherry, soy sauce and three tablespoons of water
until smooth. Add to the wok and cook until the
sauce has thickened, then add the noodles and
sesame oil. Toss everything together until heated
through and the turkey is completely cooked.

Preparation time: 15 minutes.
Cooking time: 15 minutes.
Calories per serving: 325.

Cod with a crusty herb topping

Serves 4

4 slices bread, crumbled into breadcrumbs
2 tbsp finely chopped fresh parsley
2 tbsp finely snipped fresh chives
25g/1oz finely chopped fresh tarragon
juice of 1/2 lemon
finely grated rind of 1 lemon
1 beaten egg
4 x 140g/5oz skinless cod fillets
olive oil, for sprinkling over crust
salt and pepper

FOR THE SALSA

2 green chillies, seeded and finely chopped (see
   Tip, page 155)
6 tomatoes, finely chopped
2 courgettes, finely chopped
2 tbsp finely chopped fresh coriander
3 spring onions, finely chopped
2 tbsp fresh lime juice
finely grated rind of 1 lime
4 tbsp olive oil

1 Preheat the oven to 190C/375F/Gas 5. Lightly
grease a large ovenproof dish. Make the salsa: mix
together all the ingredients, season and set aside
for the flavours to infuse.
2 In a bowl, mix together the breadcrumbs,
herbs, lemon juice and grated rind and season.
Gradually add the beaten egg and loosely bind
the mixture together.
3 Place the cod fillets in the dish, top with the
breadcrumb mixture pressing down all over to
form a thick crust, then sprinkle with olive oil.
Bake for 10-15 minutes until the topping is crisp
and brown and the fish flesh has cooked through
and turned opaque. Serve with the salsa.

Preparation time: 20 minutes.
Cooking time: 15 minutes.
Calories per serving: 464.

Chunky tuna fish cakes

Serves 2

350g/12oz mashed potato, cooled
200g can tuna, drained
3 spring onions, chopped
55g/2oz frozen sweetcorn
1 beaten egg
55g/2oz fine fresh breadcumbs
salt and freshly ground black pepper
oil, for frying
lightly fried diced cooked potatoes and fresh cress,
   to serve

1 Mix together the mashed potato, tuna, spring
onions and sweetcorn and season well. Using
your hands, shape into four fish cakes.
2 Coat with beaten egg, then dip into the
breadcrumbs. Shallow fry in hot oil for 4 minutes
on each side until golden and serve with the
potatoes and cress.

Preparation time: 30 minutes.
Cooking time: 10 minutes.
Calories per fish cake: 637.

Potato galette

Serves 4

900g/2lb potatoes
2 tbsp olive oil
2 red onions, sliced
2 garlic cloves, crushed
2 leeks, sliced
2 red peppers, halved, seeded and cut into strips
6 sun-dried tomatoes, sliced
250g pkt fresh spinach
large bunch of parsley, chopped
bunch of chives, snipped
4 eggs, beaten
25g/1oz Cheddar or Parmesan cheese, grated
salt and pepper

1 Preheat the oven to 190C/375F/Gas 5. Simmer the potatoes in boiling salted water until just tender, then drain. When cool enough to handle, evenly slice.
2 Heat the olive oil in a large frying pan and cook the onions until softened, then add the garlic. Add the leeks and fry for 2 minutes. Stir in the red pepper strips and cook for 2-3 minutes, then leave to cool slightly.
3 Arrange a layer of potatoes in the base of a deep 18cm/7in straight-sided ovenproof dish. Top with a layer of the onion and pepper mixture, a few sun-dried tomato slices and spinach leaves. Season well, then sprinkle over some parsley and chives. Repeat the layering, finishing with a layer of potatoes.
4 Season the beaten eggs and pour over the galette, making sure they seep well in. Bake for 25-30 minutes, or until the eggs set. Sprinkle over the cheese and then leave to stand for 2 minutes before serving.

Preparation time: 20 minutes.
Cooking time: 30 minutes.
Calories per serving: 330.

Red bean and tomato salsa salad

Although this salad contains avocado, the high proportion of lime means it can still be prepared well ahead of time – in fact, it enhances the delicious flavour.

Serves 6

420g can red kidney beans, drained
225g/8oz tomatoes, finely chopped
1/2 red onion, finely chopped
grated rind of 1/2 lime
juice of 2 limes
1 large firm ripe avocado, peeled, stoned and diced
2 tbsp olive oil
1 green chilli, seeded and very finely chopped (see Tip, page 155)
15g/1/2 oz very finely chopped fresh coriander
1/2 tsp salt
lime slices and fresh coriander sprigs, to garnish (optional)

1 Place all the ingredients in a bowl or rigid container as you prepare them, stir well. Chill until ready, then garnish with the lime and coriander, if using.

Preparation time: 10 minutes.
Calories per serving: 159.

TIP

For a delicious vegetarian starter, layer slices of sautéed aubergine, mozzarella, beef tomatoes, skinned yellow peppers and mixed herbs in a ring mould and place in the fridge to chill.

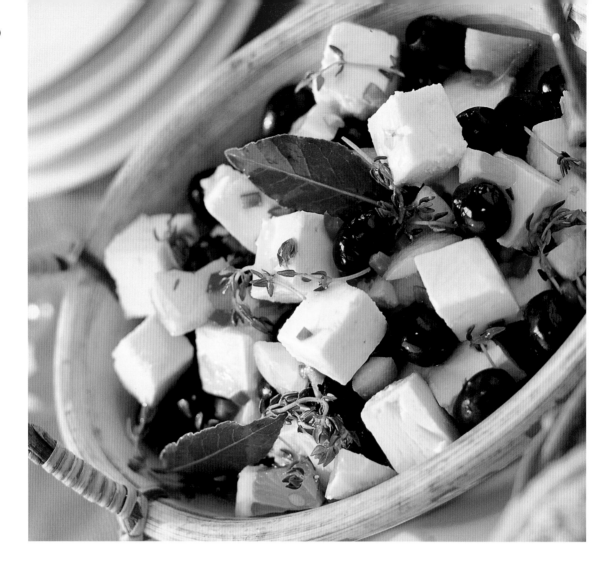

Lemon and herb marinated olives with feta

Dressed olives can be very expensive, so I find that preparing my own is much more economical – and tastier. Good quality virgin olive oil is essential for this dish, bringing richness and warmth to Mediterranean flavours. Virgin olive oil may be pricey but you can taste the difference.

Serves 4

100g/3½ oz large pitted green or black olives in
*   brine, drained*
1 small lemon, chopped
1 garlic clove, finely sliced
1 small red chilli, seeded and finely chopped (see
*   Tip, page 155)*
small bunch fresh thyme sprigs
125ml/4fl oz virgin olive oil
100g/3½ oz feta cheese, cubed
fresh bay leaves, to garnish

1 Place the olives, lemon, garlic, chilli and thyme in a bowl. Stir in the olive oil until the ingredients are coated. Gently stir in the feta cheese. Cover and chill for 8 hours or overnight. Garnish with bay leaves and serve.

Preparation time: 10 minutes, plus marinating.
Calories per serving: 348.

Savoury tatin

A tatin is the name given to a dish cooked upside down, then turned out the right way before serving. This is an excellent vegetarian dish and very easy to make.

Serves 4

85g/3oz butter
1 dsp caster sugar
12 shallots, halved
12 cherry tomatoes, halved
225g/8oz puff pastry, thawed if frozen
beaten egg and a little milk mixed together, for
  glazing
salt and pepper
fresh flatleaf parsley sprigs, to garnish

1 Heat half the butter in a thick-based pan, add the sugar and the shallots. Cook, uncovered, over a medium heat for 20 minutes until they have turned a deep brown. Stir from time to time to stop them from sticking to the bottom of the pan. If they haven't turned mahogany at the end of the cooking time, increase the heat and cook for a further 10 minutes or so.
2 Preheat the oven to 200C/400F/Gas 6. Heat the remaining butter and add the tomatoes. Cook over a medium heat for a few minutes to sear.
3 On a lightly floured surface, roll out the pastry to a 23-25cm/9-10in circle. Place a round 20cm/8in non-stick baking tin on top and, using a small sharp knife, cut round the tin.

4 Arrange the shallots and tomatoes attractively in the base of the baking tin, spoon over any pan juices and season. Cover with the pastry circle, tucking it down inside the edge of the tin so it will form a lip on the upturned tart. Glaze with the egg and milk.
5 Bake for 15 minutes or until the pastry has risen and is golden and crisp. Loosen the tatin by running a knife around the inside edge of the tin. Place a plate over the top and flip over, gently easing the tin off. Garnish and serve hot.

Preparation time: 25 minutes.
Cooking time: 15 minutes.
Calories per serving: 395.

TIPS

Caramelizing gives a lovely sweet taste to the onions. It's very important not to let the shallots burn – if they do they will become bitter.

Don't throw the pastry trimmings away, they can be used for another recipe such as jam tarts.

To complement the flavour of the tatin, serve with a mixed herb salad of coriander, parsley, torn lettuce leaves and snipped chives.

Quick kedgeree

Serves 2

1 leek, sliced
1 tbsp sunflower oil
knob of butter
225g/8oz smoked haddock
225g/8oz cooked rice
100g/3½ oz frozen peas
1-2 hard-boiled eggs, chopped

1 Fry the leek in the oil and butter until softened. Add the haddock and cook for 5 minutes. Remove skin, then break up lightly with a fork.
2 Add the rice, peas and eggs to the pan and stir fry for 5 minutes to heat through.

Preparation time: 10 minutes.
Cooking time: 10 minutes.
Calories per serving: 454.

Smoked salmon pâté

This is great on bagels or toast.

Serves 4

225g/8oz smoked salmon trimmings
200g/7oz cream cheese
1 tbsp fresh lemon juice
freshly ground pepper
few drops Tabasco sauce
2 tbsp soured cream
1 tbsp wholegrain mustard

1 Place all the ingredients in a food processor or blender and process lightly until you have a paste-like consistency. Cover and chill until needed.

Preparation time: 5 minutes.
Calories per serving: 326.

Spicy chicken tortillas

Serves 2

1 red onion, sliced
1 red pepper, halved, seeded and sliced
1 tbsp oil
250g/9oz cooked chicken, cut into strips
1½ tsp Jamaican jerk seasoning
4 ready-made flour tortillas
4 tbsp soured cream or tomato salsa or relish
4 tbsp grated cheese
4 tbsp ready-made guacamole
cayenne pepper, for sprinkling
green salad, to serve

1 Fry the onion and red pepper in the oil for 5 minutes. Add the chicken and jerk seasoning and stir fry for 5 minutes until the chicken is hot.
2 Preheat the grill to hot. Warm the tortillas, then spread each one with soured cream, tomato salsa or relish. Add the chicken mixture and roll up. Top with the grated cheese and grill briefly until just melted. Serve topped with guacamole, sprinkled with cayenne pepper, and a green salad.

Preparation time: 15 minutes.
Cooking time: 5 minutes.
Calories per serving: 873.

TIP

Treat chillies with care. Volatile oils in the seeds and flesh will sting if they come into contact with your eyes, and can cause a burning sensation on fingers. Seed chillies in a bowl, under water and wash your hands immediately afterwards. Alternatively, wear polythene gloves. Wash knives and cutting surfaces immediately you have finished.

Chicken and pasta niçoise

Serves 4

3 tbsp olive oil
2 large skinless boneless chicken breasts, cut into bite-size pieces
2 red onions, diced
2 garlic cloves, crushed
2 red chillies, seeded and diced (see Tip below)
90ml/3fl oz red wine
1 tbsp each of chopped fresh thyme and torn basil leaves, mixed together
425g can chopped tomatoes
2 courgettes, diced
55g/2oz each of pitted black and pitted green olives
675g/1½ lb tagliatelle, cooked
handful of chopped fresh parsley
salt and pepper

1 Heat the oil in large pan, add the chicken pieces and cook gently until brown all over, then, transfer to a plate. Place the onions, garlic and chillies in the pan and cook for 2 minutes or until softened. Return the chicken to the pan.
2 Stir in the wine, herbs and tomatoes and cook over a medium heat for 10 minutes or until the chicken is thoroughly cooked. Add the courgettes and olives and season to taste. Add the pasta and heat through. Stir in the parsley and serve.

Preparation time: 15 minutes.
Cooking time: 20 minutes.
Calories per serving: 625.

Thai chicken curry

Curry is now Britain's favourite dish, even outselling the traditional fish and chips. This is a healthy, low fat dish which could be prepared and marinated in advance, then cooked very simply and quickly just before serving, making it the ideal fast food for entertaining.

Serves 4

4 skinless boneless chicken breasts
4 tsp finely chopped lime rind
juice of 2 limes
1 stem lemon grass, finely chopped
3 fresh red or green chillies, seeded and chopped
  (see Tip, page 155)
2 dsp Thai fish sauce (nam pla)
bunch of fresh coriander
2 tbsp groundnut oil
2 tbsp coarsely chopped garlic
5cm/2in piece fresh root ginger, finely chopped
bunch of spring onions, finely chopped
400ml can coconut milk
jasmine or other rice, to serve

1 In a non-metallic bowl, marinate the chicken in the lime rind and juice, lemon grass, half the chillies, fish sauce and two tablespoons of chopped coriander for at least 1 hour, longer if possible.
2 Drain the chicken, reserving the marinade, and fry in half the oil for a couple of minutes to seal, then pour over the reserved marinade. Cook, over a medium heat, for 15 minutes or until the chicken is golden and thoroughly cooked through.
3 Place the remaining oil in a pan and add the garlic, ginger, remaining chillies and the spring onions. Stir fry for 2 minutes or until soft. Add half the coconut milk and bring to the boil, then pour over the chicken and heat through. Serve with the rice and garnish with remaining coriander leaves.

Preparation time: 1 hour, including marinating.
Cooking time: 20 minutes.
Calories per serving: 210.

Mango and coconut chicken with spicy potato wedges

Serves 2

2 tbsp mango chutney
squeeze of lime juice
dash of chilli sauce
1 tbsp desiccated coconut
4 chicken thighs
2 medium potatoes, cut into eight wedges
sunflower oil
paprika, mustard powder and salt, for sprinkling

1 Preheat the oven to 220C/425F/Gas 7. Mix together the mango chutney, lime juice, chilli sauce and coconut and spread over the chicken thighs. Bake in a roasting tin for 45 minutes or until the juices run clear.
2 Meanwhile, place the potato wedges on a baking tray, drizzle with oil and sprinkle with paprika, mustard powder and salt, and bake for 30 minutes alongside the chicken.

Preparation time: 10 minutes.
Cooking time: 45 minutes.
Calories per serving: 556.

TIP

Use the remaining coconut milk mixed with water to cook the rice.

New potatoes with blue cheese and crispy bacon

Quite simply, this is delicious. Toss the potatoes in the dressing while they are still slightly warm.

Serves 6

1kg/2¼ lb firm new potatoes, such as Charlottes, halved or sliced, if large
8 rashers rindless smoked streaky bacon
2 tbsp snipped fresh chives

FOR THE BLUE CHEESE DRESSING

75g/2¾ oz dolcelatte
200ml/7fl oz crème fraîche
1 tsp Dijon mustard
1 tbsp white wine vinegar
freshly ground black pepper

1 Steam or boil the potatoes for 15-20 minutes until just tender.
2 Meanwhile, dry fry the bacon until really crisp – this will take about 10 minutes.
3 Make the blue cheese dressing: mash the dolcelatte, then beat in the remaining ingredients and place in a bowl or rigid container.
4 Toss the potatoes in the dressing, then break or snip the bacon into pieces and sprinkle over. Cover and chill if making ahead. Scatter liberally with fresh chives before serving.

Preparation time: 20 minutes.
Calories per serving: 428.

TIP

If making the blue cheese dressing ahead, check its consistency as you remove it from the fridge – you may need to add a tablespoon or two of milk to return it to its creamy texture before combining with the potatoes.

Mushroom, bacon and potato gratin

Serves 4

250g/9oz new potatoes in their skins
2 tbsp olive oil
1 onion, finely diced
8 rashers rindless smoked bacon, diced
225g/8oz button mushrooms, chopped
125g/4½ oz cherry tomatoes, halved
2 tbsp chopped fresh parsley
140g/5oz farmhouse Cheddar cheese, grated
green salad, to serve

FOR THE SALAD DRESSING

4 tbsp olive oil
1 tbsp fresh lemon juice
½ tsp wholegrain mustard
salt and pepper
snipped chives

1 Make the salad dressing: whisk together all the ingredients and set aside. Cook the potatoes in boiling salted water until tender. Drain and halve.
2 Heat the oil in a frying pan, add the onion and bacon and cook for 2-3 minutes or until softened. Add the mushrooms and tomatoes, then stir in the potatoes and parsley.
3 Preheat the grill to very hot. Transfer the mixture to a shallow ovenproof dish, sprinkle over the cheese and grill until the cheese bubbles. Toss the green salad in the dressing just before serving with the gratin.

Preparation time: 10 minutes.
Cooking time: 20 minutes.
Calories per serving: 590.

TIPS

Replace the bacon with sliced leeks.

Omit the potatoes and pile the mixture on to toasted ciabatta, sprinkle with grated cheese and serve as a snack.

Spring vegetable risotto

Risotto (literally 'little rice') is a classic Italian dish. It is extremely simple to prepare and very versatile, just as good as a side dish or, with a few extra ingredients, as a main meal.

Serves 4-6

2 tbsp olive oil
25g/1oz butter
225g/8oz Arborio rice
850ml/1½ pints boiling vegetable stock
1 large courgette, sliced
140g/5oz sugar snap peas, trimmed
115g/4oz frozen baby broad beans
100g pkt asparagus tips, halved crossways
6 spring onions, finely sliced
salt and pepper
4 tbsp chopped fresh parsley or coriander
Parmesan cheese shavings, to garnish

1 Heat half the oil with the butter in a large pan, then stir in the rice until well coated. Gradually add half the stock, stirring well. Simmer until the stock has been absorbed by the rice.
2 Meanwhile, stir fry the vegetables in the remaining oil in a wok or large frying pan for about 2-3 minutes.
3 Add the remaining stock to the rice and cook until it is nearly all absorbed and has a creamy consistency. Stir occasionally. Add the vegetables to the rice and season. Transfer to a serving dish and sprinkle with the parsley. Serve garnished with the Parmesan shavings.

Preparation time: 10 minutes.
Cooking time: 20 minutes.
Calories per serving: 450.

Roast pepper salad with pine nuts and basil

A short spell in a hot oven changes the texture of peppers – they become silky and luxurious and their flavour intensifies. This dish shows them off perfectly, with the nutty flavour of pine nuts.

Serves 6

3 large red peppers, quartered and seeded
3 large yellow peppers, quartered and seeded
3 tbsp extra virgin olive oil, plus extra for brushing
1 garlic clove, crushed
1½ tbsp balsamic vinegar
2 tbsp small fresh basil leaves
3 tbsp toasted pine nuts
salt and pepper

1 Preheat the oven to 230C/450F/Gas 8. Rub or brush the peppers generously with oil, then arrange skin-side up on two oiled baking sheets. Roast for 25-30 minutes until the skins are wrinkly and quite charred.
2 Place the peppers in a plastic bag, seal and allow to cool. The steam created in the bag softens the skins, making them easier to peel. Discard the skins and place the peppers in a non-metallic bowl or rigid container with the garlic, three tablespoons of oil, the vinegar, basil leaves, pine nuts and seasoning. Cover and marinate in the fridge until ready to eat.

Preparation time: 2 hours, plus 2 hours marinating.
Calories per serving: 154.

Apricot and almond layer

Serves 4

250g/9oz fresh apricots, halved and stoned
150ml/¹/₄ pint brandy
300ml/¹/₂ pint double or whipping cream
250g tub mascarpone cheese
200g/7oz Amaretti biscuits, roughly crushed

1 Place the apricots in pan and cover with cold water. Bring to the boil, then simmer for 5 minutes. Cool slightly and skin the apricots, then place in a food processor or liquidizer and purée until smooth. Stir in two tablespoons of brandy.
2 Whip the cream until thick, then fold in the mascarpone. Drizzle the remaining brandy over the Amaretti biscuits.
3 Spoon a layer of apricot purée into the base of individual glasses or a large dish. Top with a little cream mixture and a sprinkling of Amaretti biscuits. Continue layering, finishing with the biscuits. Chill for 1 hour before serving.

Preparation time: 15 minutes.
Chilling time: 1 hour.
Calories per serving: 300.

TIPS

This apricot and almond dessert can be kept, covered, in the fridge for up to four days.

Fromage frais can be used instead of cream. It does not whip but it is thick, and lower in calories! Simply fold it into the mascarpone.

Pecan grilled plums

Sweet, fully ripe dessert plums or large greengages are best for this dessert as they are only under the grill long enough to melt the topping rather than cook the fruit.

Serves 4

55g/2oz butter, softened
4 tbsp light muscovado sugar
2 tbsp plain flour
55g/2oz chopped pecan nuts, plus extra halves
8 large ripe plums or greengages, halved and stoned
plum or damson leaves, to decorate

1 Preheat the grill to medium. Cream together the butter, sugar and flour, then stir in the chopped pecan nuts.
2 Arrange the plums, cut side up, in a large heatproof dish and spoon the pecan filling into the centres.
3 Grill for 3-5 minutes until the filling has melted and starts to brown. Top randomly with the halved pecans, grill a few seconds more until the nuts turn golden, and serve decorated with the leaves.

Preparation time: 10 minutes.
Cooking time: 6 minutes.
Calories per serving: 330.

the icing on the cake

Well, you didn't think you'd get away without my giving you a few cake ideas, did you? I've kept it to six favourites which should give you enough scope for all the year's big occasions without having to invest in any special equipment. All the designs can be easily adapted to suit your particular purpose, and, once you've got the hang of the basic techniques, you'll be able to think up plenty of your own ideas.

A home-made wedding cake is a real delight. Mixed and made with tender loving care, you can be sure that the very best ingredients are used to create a rich, mouth-watering cake and the decoration can be designed as you really want it. As the cake can be stored at every stage, you can work on it at a gentle pace over several months, to be sure that it will be ready and perfect on the day. You can also opt for doing just one or two stages, for example making just the cake and or flat icing it ready for a professional to add the decoration.

wedding *cake*

Achieving a smooth finish with royal icing is one of the most difficult stages, so we've covered this cake with ready-to-roll icing. All the icings and equipment are available from cake decorating stores.

YOU WILL NEED

1 x 15, 23, 30cm/6, 9, 12in round Rich fruit cakes (recipes page 168) · **1 x 23, 30, 38cm/9,12,15in round drum cake boards** · string, for measuring · **3.1kg/6³⁄₄ lb almond paste** · icing sugar, for dusting · **8 tbsp apricot jam, warmed and sieved** · cake icing smoother · **6 tbsp clear alcohol, such as gin** · 3.6kg/8lb ready-to-roll icing · **greaseproof paper** · 1.3kg/3lb royal icing (recipe page 169) · **no 43 and no 44 star icing nozzles** · no 2 and no 3 plain icing nozzles · **7 x 9cm/3¹⁄₂ in cake icing pillars** · 4 lengths food grade plastic dowelling · **white vegetable fat, for greasing** · 150g/5¹⁄₂ oz flower paste · **small, medium, large blossom cutters** · ball-shaped modelling tool · **kitchen foil** · pink, yellow and green edible dusting powders · **cream paste food colouring** · small, medium and large ivy cutters · **1 pkt each white and green florist's wire** · florist's tape · **3m x 5mm/3¹⁄₂ yd x ⁵⁄₈ in wide satin ribbon**

STORING

To store an uncut iced tier of a wedding cake, place in a large cardboard box and leave in a cool, dark place. Do not store in a sealed airtight container. A cake kept this way will last for up to two years. The icing may discolour after such a long time, so it is best to remove it along with the almond paste and re-decorate later, but the cake itself should still taste absolutely delicious.

Rich fruit cake

This cake is at its best four months after baking. Use the chart opposite to determine the specific tin size and the ingredient quantities. You can add ground mixed spice, orange or lemon rind, vanilla or almond essence or orange or lemon juice to taste. If you prefer not to use nuts, glacé cherries or mixed peel, add extra weight to one of the other ingredients. The baking times include the initial 30 minutes baking.

1 Preheat the oven to 150C/300F/Gas 2. Grease the cake tin and line the base and sides with a double layer of greaseproof paper.

2 Use a large, clean washing-up bowl for mixing the bigger cakes. Halve, rinse and dry the cherries, then place in the bowl. Add the flour, currants, sultanas, raisins, mixed peel, nuts and ground spice, if using. Mix all the ingredients together well.

3 Cream together the butter and caster sugar until light and fluffy, then gradually beat in the eggs. Add orange or lemon rind to taste, if you like. Stir this creamed mixture into the fruit and flour mixture and continue stirring until everything is well combined.

4 Transfer the mixture to the tin, then level the top with the back of a spoon. Place the tin on a baking sheet and bake in the centre of the oven for 30 minutes, then reduce the oven temperature to 140C/275F/Gas 1 and continue baking for the remaining time in the chart. (Check to see if the cake is done 30 minutes before the end of the recommended baking time.) When the cake is cooked it should feel firm and have begun to shrink from the sides of the tin. When a skewer is inserted in the centre it should come out clean. Leave to cool completely in the tin or place on a wire rack.

5 When the cake is completely cool, remove it from the tin, but leave the lining paper on as this helps to keep it moist. Turn the cake upside down and wrap it in another layer of greaseproof paper, then cover loosely with foil. Store the cake upside down in a cool, dark place.

6 To improve the flavour, pierce the cake all over with a cocktail stick or fine skewer and pour over a little brandy at monthly intervals. Re-wrap and store as before.

Ingredients, baking times and icing quantities for rich fruit cake	Round tin	15cm/6in	23cm/9in	30cm/12in
	glacé cherries	70g/2½ oz	140g/5oz	350g/12oz
	plain flour	175g/6oz	300g/10½ oz	750g/1lb 10oz
	currants	140g/5oz	280g/10oz	675g/1½ lb
	sultanas	215g/7½ oz	425g/15oz	1kg/2¼ lb
	raisins	70g/2½ oz	140g/5oz	350g/12oz
	mixed peel	55g/2oz	85g/3oz	175g/6oz
	chopped nuts	25g/1oz	85g/3oz	175g/6oz
	butter	140g/5oz	280g/10oz	675g/1½ lb
	caster sugar	140g/5oz	280g/10oz	675g/1½ lb
	medium eggs	3	5	12
	Baking times	3¾ hours	4½ hours	5 hours
	Almond paste			
	3.1kg/6¾ lb	550g/1¼ lb	1.1kg/2½ lb	1.3kg/3lb
	Ready-roll icing			
	3.6kg/8lb	675g/1½ lb	1.3kg/3lb	1.6kg/3½ lb

Assembling and preparing the cake for decoration

1 Place each cake on a board. Using a piece of string, measure the top and sides of each cake as one measurement. Divide the almond paste into three pieces (see chart) and lightly dust a work surface with icing sugar. Brush each cake with warm apricot jam. Roll out each almond paste piece to a circle, the diameter equal to the length of string. Drape almond paste over each cake. Smooth over the top and sides with the palm of your hand or use a cake icing smoother if you have one and trim the edges. Leave to dry for 24-48 hours.
2 Brush each cake with clear alcohol. Lightly dust a work surface with icing sugar. Divide the ready-to-roll icing into three pieces (see chart). Roll out each icing piece to a circle large enough to cover each cake. (Re-measure cakes with the string.) Drape icing over each cake. Smooth down with the palm of your hand or use a cake icing smoother, rubbing the top and sides of the cake until smooth – this also helps to make a neat, straight edge.
3 Dampen the edge of each cake board. If necessary, knead together icing trimmings and roll out three 7.5cm/3in wide long strips of icing and place around each cake board to cover. Smooth out any creases and trim to fit.

ROYAL ICING

This quantity makes enough to cover a three-tier wedding cake. As an alternative, you can use a packet of royal icing mix. Look out for pasteurized egg white sold in cake decorating stores.

YOU WILL NEED

6 egg whites (or 7½ tsp egg albumen)
• 1.3kg/3lb icing sugar • 3 tsp glycerine

1 Beat egg whites lightly with a fork, or dissolve the albumen according to the packet instructions. Gradually whisk in the icing sugar until it is smooth and forms soft peaks.
2 Beat in glycerine. Keep covered to stop crystals forming.

Decorating the cake

Before you start to ice the cake, measure the circumference of each cake. Cut 5cm/2in wide strips of greaseproof paper to exact lengths. Divide the paper into nine equal spaces for the small cake, 12 spaces for the medium cake and 15 spaces for the large cake. (These are a length guide for piping the scrolls.) Wrap the paper around the cake and mark the top and bottom edges of the cake with a pin prick to indicate where the spaces are. Remove paper.

1 To pipe the top edges: place royal icing in a piping bag fitted with the no 44 star nozzle. For each 'S' scroll, start just over the edge of the cake and pipe in a continuous swirling action. Make it thick at the top of the scroll and taper it slightly at the end to give a long tail. Repeat the 'S' scrolls all round the top of each of the three cakes.

2 Using the no 43 star nozzle, overpipe with a straight line on top of each scroll. Then pipe two more straight lines on top of each scroll, using first the no 3 plain nozzle, then the no 2 plain nozzle.

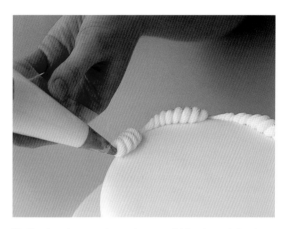

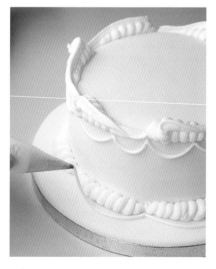

3 To ice the side of the cake: tilt it away from you by placing a wedge under the front edge. Using first the no 3 plain nozzle, then the no 2 plain nozzle, pipe two semi-circles just below each 'S' scroll. To pipe the bottom edges: use the no 44 star nozzle to pipe loops of icing in a 'C' shape between each section. Start with a thinner loop at the point of each 'C' scroll, making it fatter in the centre and thinner at the end.

4 Using first the no 3 plain nozzle, then the no 2 plain nozzle, pipe semi-circles of icing one on top of the other, very close to the 'C' scroll.

Making the open roses and ivy

The delicate colour of the flowers and leaves adds the finishing touch to this cake. Keep the flower paste covered at all times with plastic film to prevent drying and roll out only one flower at a time.

To make open roses: lightly grease a work surface with white vegetable fat. Roll out a small piece of flower paste very thinly. Cut out flowers using the blossom cutters. You will need to make nine large blossoms, seventeen medium blossoms and eight small blossoms. Place flowers in the palm of your hand and roll edges with a modelling tool until they frill and 'cup' lightly. Place in a cup of foil and leave to dry for 24 hours. Dust the edges very lightly with pink dusting powder. Assemble nine large and nine medium blossoms together and eight small and eight medium blossoms together, secured

with a dot of royal icing to make seventeen roses. Roll out small pea shapes of ready-to-roll icing, dust with yellow powder and place in the centre of each flower, secured with royal icing. Leave flowers to dry or two days.

To make ivy: colour the remaining flower paste with cream colouring and roll out a little at a time on a work surface lightly greased with white fat. Using the three cutter sizes, cut out about 142 leaves and allow to dry for 24 hours. Pipe a dot of royal icing on the back of each leaf and attach a short length of white florist's wire to each one. Leave to dry. Wind florist's tape around the green wires, taping in each leaf as you work down the stems. Finally, dust each leaf with green dusting powder. Make about fifteen stems in all, each with about eight to ten leaves on.

Assembling the floral decoration

Place a small ball of ready-to-roll icing in the centre of each cake and arrange five roses in the centre of the small cake, six roses on the medium cake and six on the large cake. Then arrange the ivy stems around them. Secure with royal icing. Wrap satin ribbon around the edges of the cake boards and secure with a dab of royal icing.

5 To complete the top: using first the no 3 plain nozzle, then the no 2 plain nozzle, pipe semi-circles of icing one on top of the other, very close to the 'S' scrolls.

6 Position the pillars on top of the large and medium cakes and mark positions with a pin prick. Push each piece of cake dowelling down through the cake, marking the top edge of the cake with a pencil. Remove dowelling and cut so that it is flush with the top of the cake. Replace in the cakes.

Make this terracotta window box cake bursting with jasmine, petunias and ivy. The 'pot' is simply covered with almond paste and the flowers can be made weeks in advance.

If you have never worked with sugar or flower paste before, the flowers will take a little practice. You could easily use silk flowers for a quicker effect, and if you don't want to go to the expense of buying the fruit and flower swag mould, simply roll out sausages of almond paste and score on a pattern with a cocktail stick. This rich fruit cake will keep for several months in a cool, dry room.

YOU WILL NEED

25cm/10in square Rich fruit cake (recipe page 168) • **icing sugar, for dusting** • 1.5kg/3lb 5oz almond paste • **5 tbsp apricot jam, warmed and sieved** • paprika, chestnut, holly green, spruce green, cream and black paste colours • **fruit and flower swag mould, (optional)** • cornflour, for dusting • **fleur-de-lys mould, (optional)** • small artist's paint brush • **40cm/16in square cake board** • 500g/1lb 2oz sugar paste

For the flowers and leaves

1 pkt each 26 and 28 gauge florist's wire • **350g/12oz flower paste** • small, medium and large ivy cutters • **1 egg white, beaten** • superwhite icing whitener • **florist's tape** • green, brown, pink, red food powders • **small calyx cutter** • cocktail sticks or modelling tool • **wooden dowelling** • 4cm/1½in plain round cutter • **14 posy pricks**

blooming
marvellous

Jasmine template

Petunia template

Making the base

1 Cut the cake into two 25 x 13cm/10 x 5in rectangles. Lightly sprinkle a work surface with icing sugar, then roll out 100g/3½ oz of almond paste to a 25 x 13cm/10 x 5in rectangle. Spread one half of the cake with warm jam, top with almond paste and sandwich with the other cake half.

From three-quarters of the way up the sides, trim the cake on all sides downwards and inwards to shape the base of the terracotta pot. Using a serrated knife, trim the top of the cake to give a rounded shape similar to a loaf of bread. Spread all over with warm apricot jam.

2 Knead paprika and chestnut food colourings into the remaining almond paste to achieve a terracotta colour. Reserve about 150g/5½ oz, and roll out the rest to a rectangle large enough to cover the cake. Lift over the cake and press over the top and sides. Smooth out the corners and trim the edges.

3 Roll two-thirds of the reserved almond paste into a long thin sausage and press around the terracotta pot about two-thirds of the way up, to make a rim.

4 Make six flower swags: dust the mould very lightly with cornflour, press a small sausage of almond paste into the mould, then press down well. Ease out and trim. Moisten the back of the swags with a little water and press on to the cake sides, beneath the rim. Make two fleur-de-lys using the mould and attach to the cake. Paint the cake top with holly green food colouring for the 'soil'.

Making paving

Carefully lift the cake off the board. Roll out the sugar paste to a square the same size as the cake board, moisten the board and place the icing on top. Mark the icing with the back of a knife to create a crazy paving effect all over, then paint with cream, chestnut and black paste colours. Replace the cake in the centre.

Making the flowers and leaves

Cut twenty six and twenty-eight gauge wires into 7.5cm/3in lengths. Bend the top of each wire to make a tiny hook. Cut flower paste into five equal pieces and wrap tightly in food wrap to prevent drying. Make the flowers and leaves up to one month in advance and store in a cardboard box in a dry place.

Ivy Knead a little cream colouring into one piece of flower paste. Roll out a small piece at a time and cut out leaves using three different sizes of cutter. Using twenty-eight gauge wires, dip the hooked end of each wire into a tiny drop of egg white and, holding the leaf between finger and thumb, push the hooked end firmly into the icing. Mark the veins with the back of a knife. Leave to dry. Make forty of each size. When dry, mix a little spruce green with superwhite and paint leaves, then add more

green to darken and paint over the top. When dry, tape two leaves together, one slightly higher than the other, twisting the florist's tape tightly around the wires to join. As you wind the tape down the wire add another leaf, twisting the tape around about 1cm/½ in from the base of the leaf. Continue twisting the tape down the wire, adding different sizes of leaves to make about eight trailing bunches. Hold over a lightly steaming kettle for a second or two to give a gloss, if liked.

Petunia leaves Trace the leaf templates (page 172), and cut out of thin card. Colour two pieces of flower paste with a mix of holly and spruce colouring. Thinly roll out a little at a time and cut out leaves. Dip hooked ends of twenty-eight gauge wires in egg white and insert as before. Mark veins with the back of a knife. Make twenty-five leaves of each size. Leave to dry, wire together as for ivy, then steam, if liked.

Ivy, petunia and summer jasmine leaves made sugar paste.

Summer jasmine leaves Trace and cut out template (page 172). Add a little superwhite plus a hint of cream colouring to petunia leaf trimmings, to achieve a paler green. Cut out fifty leaves and insert wire as before. Twist leaves slightly to give a curled effect and leave to dry. Dust with green and brown powders. Using florist's tape, wire together in groups of five, starting with one leaf at the top, then two pairs of leaves (see diagram right). Make ten sprays. Steam, if liked.

Jasmine flowers Take a piece of white flower paste the size of a pea and roll into a pear shape. Flatten the thicker end to make a Mexican hat shape with a very thin stem. Place the calyx cutter over the top and cut out the flower. Hold the stem between finger and thumb and press a cocktail stick into the centre of the flower to make the 'throat', then press the stick against the centre of each petal to mark it. Roll each side of the petal lightly with the cocktail stick to thin it a little. Dip the hooked end of a twenty-six gauge wire in egg white and place through the flower until the hook is out of sight. Make forty flowers. To make buds, roll a little piece of flower paste into tiny pear shapes and push wires through. Make six buds. Wire the flowers and buds together with florist's tape to make about eight bunches.

Petunias Make Mexican hat shapes as above, but use a slightly larger ball of paste. Using a piece of dowelling or an artist's paint brush, roll the edge of the Mexican hat very thinly. Place a 4cm/1½ in plain cutter over the top of the hat to cut a neat circle. Turn the hat the other way up, and roll the edge of the hat very thinly with a cocktail stick. Place the point of the stick towards the centre of the hat, and roll with your index finger until the icing frills slightly. Repeat all around the petal. Hold the stem of the flower between your fingers, and press the point of a cocktail stick or modelling tool into the centre and roll around to open the centre into a trumpet shape. Make ten to twelve flowers. Mark five equally spaced veins on each flower with a cocktail stick. Dip the hooked end of a twenty-six gauge wire into egg white and push through the centre of each flower. Hang upside down to dry. (Hook the other end over the handle of a pan to support.) When dry, dust with pink and red powder colours, and, if liked, paint the 'throat' with a deeper shade. Add a dot of green in the very centre. Steam, if liked.

Assembling the cake

Gather the leaves and flowers together into fourteen groups. Push posy pricks, evenly spaced, into the 'soil', then insert bunches of flowers and leaves. Bend wires out to arrange the flowers to give a pleasing effect, making sure you cover all of the cake.

This is one of my favourite cakes. The pumpkin is so realistic, the characters around it so gruesome, and it is so easy to make. It's perfect for children's parties, of course, but it also makes an excellent table centre for an adult party, too. And any trick or treaters that come banging on your door will be very impressed if you can offer them a slice of this creepy cake. While you mix the cake, you can get the imaginative minds and nimble figures of your children to create these and other monsters to decorate the board. Have fun.

hallowe'en *cake*

YOU WILL NEED

4 x 20cm/8in round sponge cakes (recipe page 178) • 115g/4oz raspberry jam • butter cream (recipe page 178) • 1.5kg/3lb 5oz ready-to-roll icing coloured with concentrated paste food colours: 675g/1½ lb tangerine, 85g/3oz green, 400g/14oz black, 175g/6oz grey, 55g/2oz red and remainder left white (excess can be coloured to make into 'characters') • fishbone tool (optional) • 1 fine and 1 thick artist's paint brush • tangerine, brown, green, black, red concentrated paste food colours • 30cm/12in square, thick cake board • 175g/6oz icing sugar, sifted • 1 egg white • greaseproof paper piping bag • 1 wooden skewer

Sponge cakes

Makes 4 x 20cm/8in sponges

450g/1lb soft margarine
450g/1lb caster sugar
450g/1lb self-raising flour
4 tsp baking powder
8 eggs
2 tsp vanilla essence

1 Preheat the oven to 180C/350F/Gas 4. Line the bases of four 20cm/8in round, straight-sided sponge tins or spring-release cake tins. Or cook in batches.

2 Place all the ingredients in a bowl and beat for 1 minute or until light and fluffy. Divide between the tins and bake for 30 minutes. Turn out and cool on a wire rack.

Butter cream

Enough to fill and cover cake

350g/12oz butter, softened
700g/1lb 9oz icing sugar, sifted
2 tsp vanilla essence

1 Beat ingredients together with a little boiling water until you achieve the consistency of thick cream.

Assembling the cake

1 Layer the four sponge cakes with raspberry jam and butter cream, then chill. Using a sharp knife, cut the cake into a football shape. Use trimmings to fill any gaps. Coat the whole cake thinly with butter cream to prevent crumbling, chill, then give a second thick coat of butter cream. Chill for 30 minutes to firm up.

2 Lightly dust a work surface with icing sugar and roll out tangerine icing to a circle large enough to cover the top and sides of the cake. Drape over and, using the palms of your hands, mould the icing and smooth out any creases. Trim the base. Mark indents up the pumpkin using a fishbone tool or the back of a knife.

3 Paint the pumpkin with tangerine and brown food colourings to achieve a streaky effect. Make a thick stalk from 55g/2oz of the green icing and score with a knife. Press on top of the pumpkin, securing with water, if necessary, then paint with green and brown colourings. Roll out 225g/8oz of black icing and cover the board. Place pumpkin centred and towards the back of the board.

4 Paint on the mouth and teeth using black food colouring. Cut three triangles from the pumpkin for the eyes and nose. Roll out black icing and cut three triangles the same size, then insert into the holes. Press into position and secure with water, if necessary. Mix the icing sugar and egg white together to make royal icing of a piping consistency, then pipe spiders' webs on to the board.

Witch

1 Use 55g/2oz of black icing to make a cone. Thinly roll out more black icing and cut a wedge for the cloak. Drape around the body, trim to fit.

2 Place a wooden skewer through the body with 2.5cm/1in above to attach the head. (Remove the skewer before serving. If liked, make the witch from marzipan.) Make a thin cone of green icing for the head and bend the chin upwards slightly. Add a nose and two tiny white eyes, securing with a damp brush and water, if necessary. Paint the pupils red and mark wrinkles by the eyes, then paint on the mouth. Use a tiny piece of white icing for the tooth and black food colouring to paint the eyebrows.

3 Make a small cone of black icing for the hat, bending the point. Cut out a small circle of icing for the brim and position on top of the head. Place the black cone on top. Roll out long, thin sausages of red icing for the hair, cut and press under the hat.

Skewer the head on to the body. Roll out two sausages of black icing for arms, bend into shape and press on to the body. Flatten two small ovals of green icing for the hands and cut out fingers. Paint the nails red, press on to the ends of the arms, then place the witch on the board.

Gravestones, ghost and spiders

Roll and cut out two gravestones from grey icing and paint RIP with black food colouring. Leave to dry overnight. Make the ghost: mould white icing into a ghost shape, then drape behind gravestone. Paint on facial features. Make the spiders: use black icing and roll out thin sausages for legs, sticking in place with water. Use white icing and black food colouring for eyes.

Specially decorated cakes really make a birthday whatever the age, and to see the look of surprise and delight on a child's face, reflected in the candlelight, is magic.

Of course, for Mums it's a bit of a nightmare deciding what to do. So, here are two cakes, one for a boy and one for a girl, with an easy decoration around the side and decorations on top that leave room for a ring of candles. If you are short of time you can always buy a ready-made, flat iced cake from your local supermarket which leaves you with more time to add the decoration.

children's
birthday
cakes

FOR EACH CAKE YOU WILL NEED

20cm/8in round sponge cake filled and covered with a thin layer of butter cream (recipes page 178), or 20cm/8in round fruit cake covered with marzipan • **28cm/11in round drum cake board** • icing sugar, for dusting • **900g/2lb white ready-to-roll icing** • cake icing smoother (optional) • **greaseproof paper icing bag (optional)** • 55g/2oz royal icing • **small shell piping nozzle (optional)**

FOR THE DECORATION (see individual cakes)

white ready-to-roll icing • **paste food colourings** • string, for measuring, and a cocktail stick • **writing guides (optional)** • no 1 writing tube (optional), or an artist's fine paint brush

Preparing each cake for decoration

Place the cake in the centre of the cake board. Lightly dust a work surface with icing sugar. Roll out the icing to a circle large enough to cover the top of the cake and down the sides. Drape the icing over the cake and smooth down with the palm of your hand or use a cake icing smoother, rubbing the top and sides of the cake until smooth – this also helps to make a neat, straight edge. Trim the base with a sharp knife and reserve all trimmings. Pipe small royal icing shells around the base. After piping shells, colour remaining icing for your greeting. Keep covered with food wrap, until needed.

Making the swags

Knead a little food colouring into the icing trimmings, see Icing tips, page 183. Roll out thinly and cut into six 15cm/6in long x 1cm/½ in wide strips. Measure around the cake with string, then mark the top edge into six equal sections with a cocktail stick. Lightly twist each strip and secure in loops around the side of the cake. Use water to stick in place. Hold each swag in position for a few seconds before adding the next. To finish the swags, see individual cakes.

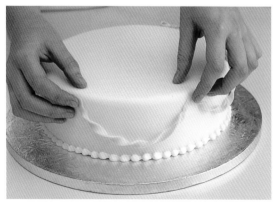

Ballet cake

YOU WILL NEED

360g/12½oz white ready-to-roll icing • **pink paste food colouring** • 1 ready-iced cake with six pink swags (page 181) •
small knife • pink royal icing, for greeting, and little shoe bows • **candles (optional)**

1 Make the bows: reserve 60g/2¼ oz of icing and wrap in plastic film. Knead a little pink food colouring into the remaining icing until pale pink. Roll out 100g/3½ oz pink icing and cut six 7.5 x 1cm/3 x ½ in strips and six 1cm x 5mm/½ x ¼ in strips for the centres of the bows. To fold each bow, take the ends of a larger strip, fold over to the centre and secure ends with a little water. As you do so, push the folded end upwards so that it forms a loop.

2 Place a smaller strip of icing across the join to represent the knot. Seal at the back with a little water. Re-roll trimmings and cut into 1cm/½ in wide strips for the bow ribbons. Cut into 12 x 5cm/2in lengths and trim diagonally at one end. Attach two bow ribbons at the top of each swag and stick a bow above them.

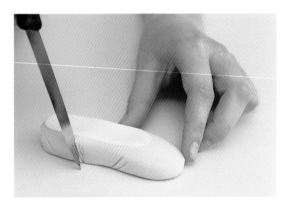

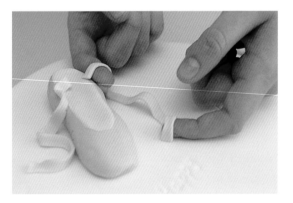

3 Make the ballet shoes: using 100g/3½ oz pink icing for each shoe, mould each piece into a 10cm/4in sausage shape. Flatten slightly and smooth round the edges with the palm of your hand. For the insides of the shoes, make an indentation along two-thirds of the top of each shoe. Roll out half the reserved white icing, cut into two long, oval strips and smooth into the indentations to give the effect of inside lining. Using the back of a small knife, mark little creases around the base of the shoes.

4 Position each shoe on top of the cake and secure with a little water. Using the remaining white icing, roll out thinly and cut out four long, thin strips. Secure one either side of each shoe with water and drape over the cake to resemble ribbons, then pipe tiny pink bows on to the front of the shoes. Write your greeting, see Icing tips opposite, and add candles.

ICING TIPS

• It is easier to make small quantities of royal icing using packet mixes.

• Always use paste food colourings for large quantities of ready-to-roll icing. For pale shades, break off a walnut-sized piece of icing and knead in a little food colouring on a surface that has been lightly sprinkled with sifted icing sugar. Break off small pieces of the coloured icing and knead into the white until the required shade is achieved. Keep all icing wrapped when it is not in use to prevent it from drying out.

• You can buy ready-to-roll icing in a selection of colours at specialist cake shops and bakeries.

• Writing your greeting. If using writing guides, select your greeting, position on top of the cake and press into the soft icing. Carefully remove the guide, colour a little royal icing, then pipe over the design using the no 1 writing tube. You can also paint the words freehand using a fine brush and paste food colour.

• To add a name to the cake, write it on paper. Use a pin to prick through the letters on to the icing before piping or painting.

• When painting directly on to icing, it is wise to check colours and practise your technique first on a piece of paper.

Rocket cake

YOU WILL NEED

175g/6oz white ready-to-roll icing • **blue, red, black, yellow and orange paste food colourings** • small star cutter • **1 ready-iced cake with six red swags (page 181)** • paint brush • **red royal icing, for greeting** • candles (optional)

1 Colour 100g/3½ oz icing blue, 50g/1¾ oz red and the remaining black. Thinly roll out 25g/1oz of blue icing. Cut out six star shapes, leave them to dry, then stick one at the top of each swag with royal icing or water.

2 Make the rocket: mould the remainder of the blue icing into a sausage shape about 9cm/3½ in long. Flatten the top of the sausage and smooth it with the palm of your hand to make the main body of the rocket. Make the rocket's nose, using half the red icing. Shape it into a triangle, then smooth into shape, making sure that the base of the nose is just a little wider than the actual width of the rocket.

3 Roll out the remaining red icing and cut out two long triangles for the wings, a small circle for the window and a half circle to fit the base of the rocket. Gather up all the scraps and cut a small rocket shape piece for the door. Cut a small circle using the black icing and stick on top of the red window and secure to the rocket. Place the rocket into position on the cake and stick all the pieces down with a little water. Mould the remaining black icing into two fat circles and position at the back of the rocket to represent the engines.

4 Paint the rocket flame: use the yellow and orange food colouring to paint on the fire radiating out of the base of the rocket. Write your greeting, see Icing tips, and add candles

It's amazing how changing the shape of a cake can make it look special. This Christmas tree cake is a real favourite, partly because it is easy to make and it doesn't require a specially shaped cake tin. It is simply cut out of a 25cm/10in square fruit cake. We chose to decorate simply with gold and silver icing baubles and bows but you could personalize yours by icing the names of your family on the parcels around the tree. Remember that gold and silver colourings are not edible and should be removed from the cake before serving.

christmas *tree* cake

Rich fruit cake

Makes 1 x 25 cm/10in square cake

550g/1¼ lb butter
550g/1¼ lb caster sugar
10 eggs, beaten
550g /1¼ lb plain flour
550g/1¼ lb currants
800g/1¾ lb sultanas
280g/10oz raisins
115g/4oz chopped nuts
115g/4oz mixed peel
225g/8oz glacé cherries, halved
grated rind and juice of 1 lemon
1 tsp mixed spice

Making the cake

1 Preheat the oven to 150C/300F/Gas 2. Grease a 25cm/10in square tin and line the base and sides with a double layer of greaseproof paper.
2 Beat the butter and sugar in a large mixing bowl until light and fluffy. Gradually beat in the eggs, a little at a time, adding a little flour if the mixture starts to curdle.
3 Add the fruit, nuts, peel, cherries, lemon rind and juice, flour and mixed spice. Fold into the mixture to give a soft dropping consistency. Transfer to the tin and then level with the back of a spoon.
4 Place the cake just below the centre of the oven and bake for 30 minutes, then reduce the temperature to 140C/275F/Gas 1 and bake for 4½-5 hours. When cooked, the cake should be firm, golden and a skewer inserted into the centre should come out clean.
5 Leave to cool in the tin overnight, then turn out, leaving on the greaseproof paper, and wrap in foil. Store for up to 3 months. The cake can be pricked occasionally and brandy drizzled over, re-wrap well.

Assembling and decorating

icing sugar, for dusting
225g/8oz ready-to-roll icing
    coloured with concentrated
    blue paste food colouring
50 x 15cm/20 x 16in cake
    board
25cm/10in square Rich fruit
    cake (recipe 184)
6 tbsp apricot jam, warmed
    and sieved
1.3kg/3lb almond paste
2.25kg/5lb ready-to-roll icing
fishbone tool or knife
silver and gold dusting powder
    or silver and gold liquid
    food colouring
fine paint brush
star cutter

1 Lightly dust the work surface with icing sugar. Roll out the dark blue icing and dampen the cake board slightly. Place the icing on the board and trim edges.

2 Cut the cake into a triangle and use corners to cut out a bucket and tree trunk. Trim the tree edges to make a rounded cone shape and round off the bucket and trunk edges. Brush all pieces with jam. Reserve trimmings for the parcels.

Lightly dust the work surface with icing sugar. Roll out three-quarters of the almond paste to cover the tree. Drape over and trim edges. Cover the trunk and bucket with almond paste and use any remaining for the parcels.

Place the tree on the board, sticking it in place with warm apricot jam. Add the trunk and bucket, joining together with more jam. Brush the whole cake very lightly with a brush dampened with water.

3 Lightly dust the work surface with icing sugar. Roll out 450g/1lb of icing and cover the trunk and bucket, drape over the top and sides and smooth down using the palms of your hands.

Roll out 900g/2lb of icing to about 5mm/¼ in thick. Cut into 7.5cm/3in long triangles. Soften two edges with your fingers and score lines down to the point, using a fishbone tool or the back of a knife. Start at the base of the tree and stick on rows of triangles, overlapping as you go. Blend the top edge of each triangle into the cake to flatten and curl the points up slightly.

Use the remaining icing for the decorations and finishing touches.

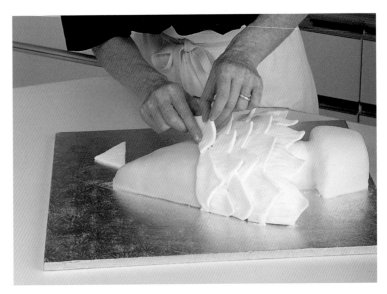

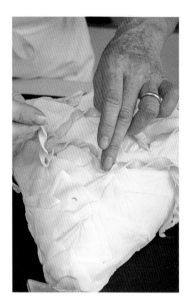

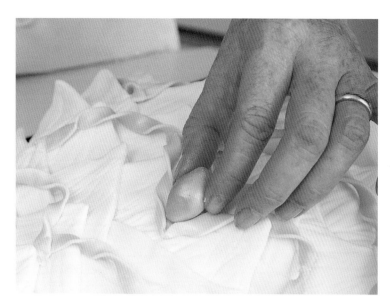

4 Make the garlands: thinly roll out icing to a 50 x 13cm/20 x 5in strip, then cut into 5mm/¼ in wide strips. Dust or paint both sides with gold, twist gently and place on the cake, securing with a damp brush. Place a bow at joins.

5 Make the baubles: roll 10 small balls of white icing and 10 ovals. Dust half with silver and half with gold powder or paint with gold and silver liquid colouring, if you prefer.

Make the bows: thinly roll out a strip of icing 6 x 13cm/2½ x 5in and cut into 10 x 5mm/¼ in wide strips. Dampen the middle of each strip and fold both ends into the centre. Wrap a shorter strip of icing over the centre and secure with water to finish bows. Make about 10 bows. Paint or dust with gold and silver.

6 Make the large bow for the bucket: roll out icing and cut a 2.5 x 25cm/1 x 10in strip. Lay over the centre of the bucket, then paint or dust with gold. Roll out icing, then cut out two 2.5 x 7.5cm/1 x 3in strips. Cut a 'V' out of one end of each strip to resemble the ribbon ends of a bow. Place in the centre of the bucket, on top of the gold strip and paint or brush with gold.

Roll out and cut a 5 x 13cm/2 x 5in icing strip and shape slightly so that the centre is narrow and the loops are curved. Fold the two ends into the centre. Cover join with an icing strip and paint or dust gold. Pack bow loops with crumpled kitchen paper to support the loops until dry.

Finishing touches

Cut the remaining fruit cake into small squares, rectangles or circles. Cover with marzipan and icing and decorate with gold and silver bows, or dust and paint. Arrange around the base of the tree.

Roll out a small piece of icing to make the Christmas star, cut out using a star cutter and paint or dust with silver colouring.

INDEX

ACKNOWLEDGEMENTS

Before it became a book, Good Living started as a magazine and then went on to develop into a television series, and I owe a huge debt of gratitude to all those involved in both projects, especially Nick Chapman, Seamus Geoghegan, Mitzie Wilson, Liz Barron, John Wiston, Liz Warner, Ben Frow, Fiona Wright, Anna Beattie and Ann Stirk.

My thanks too to Viv Bowler for the enthusiasm that she has shown in getting this book off the ground; to Bridget Hetzel for her skill and for working so extraordinarily hard to pull all the elements together, and, of course, to the experts who have taught me so much and whose contributions make the books so special:

CAKES MADE BY:
Mark Knight: Hallowe'en cake pp176-9; Children's birthday cakes pp180-3
Wendy Mills: Wedding cake pp166-71; Christmas tree cake pp184-7
Susie Spiller: Blooming marvellous pp172-5

DESIGNS
Jane Asher: Wedding cake pp166-71; Blooming marvellous pp172-5; Hallowe'en cake pp176-9; Children's birthday cakes pp180-3; Christmas tree cake pp184-7
Bridget Hetzel: Découpage plates pp42-5
Caroline Kelley: Mosaic tabletop pp46-9; Picture frames pp70-3
Melinda While: Papier mâché bowls pp74-7
Robert Wyatt and Angela Dukes: Decorative lampshades pp66-9

FEATURES
Fiona Barnett: Frosted rose wreath p116; Fruits and bay p126; Winter snow p128; Citrus slice p129
Tessa Eveleigh: Aromatic herbs pp134-7
Joanna Farrow: Chocolate mille feuille p34; Iced pudding p38; Christmas crackers p.38
Hilary More: Shoe box storage pp78-81
Hayley Newstead: Unusual flower pots pp110-13
Sue Russell: Winter warming displays pp130-3

HOME ECONOMISTS:
Sarah Buenfeld: French tarts pp10-15; Plum and caramelised almond pavlova p37; Coconut meringue ice p37; Christmas party pp102-7; Sweet chilli chicken p145; New potatoes with blue cheese and crispy bacon p159; Roast pepper salad p161; Pecan grilled plums p162
Justine Dickenson: Summer lunch party pp92-7; Marinated olives with feta p150
Joanna Farrow: Hallowe'en party pp98-101; Spring wedding pp84-91; Pies and pastries pp16-21
Janice Murfitt: Gourmet gifts pp28-33
Bridget Sargeson: Chunky tuna fishcakes p146

Anne Stirk: Turkey chow mein p145; Cod with a crusty herb topping p146; Potato galette p148; Savoury tatin p151; Smoked salmon pâté p152; Chicken and pasta niçoise p155; Thai chicken curry p156; Mushroom, potato and bacon gratin p159; Spring vegetable risotto p160; Apricot and almond layer p162
Sunil Vijayakar: Chocolate mille feuille p34; Iced pudding p38; Christmas crackers p.38

ILLUSTRATIONS
Tig Sutton: Covered shelving pp58-61

PHOTOGRAPHERS
William Adams Lingwood: Gourmet gifts pp28-33; Children's birthday cakes pp180-3; Christmas tree cake pp184-7
Mark Asher: Gorgeous gateaux (step-by-step photographs) pp22-7; Shoe box storage (main photograph) pp78-81
Martin Brigdale: Gorgeous gateaux (main photo) pp22-7; Spring wedding pp84-91; Summer lunch party pp92-7; Marinated olives with feta p150; Wedding cake (main photo) pp166-71; Blooming marvellous pp172-5
Linda Burgess: French tarts pp10-15; Plum and caramelised almond pavlova p37; Coconut meringue ice p37; Cross stitch picture pp54-7; Door wreaths p116 and pp118-19; Hand-tied gift bouquet pp120-3; Dried flower topiary pp122-5; Pecan grilled plums p163
Jean Cazals: Christmas party pp102-7
Ken Field: Recipes to impress pp8-9; Chocolate mille feuille p34; Iced pudding p38; Christmas crackers p38; Home work pp40-1; Découpage plates (step-by-step photographs) pp42-5; Mosaic tabletop (step-by-step photographs) pp46-9; Canvas embroidery cushion pp50-3; Covered shelving pp58-61; Drawstring bags pp62-5; Decorative lampshades pp66-9; Picture frames pp70-3; Papier mâché bowls pp74-7; Hallowe'en party pp98-101; Fruit pyramid pp132-3; Candlelit tray p135

Gus Filgate: Découpage plates (main photograph) pp42; Mosaic tabletop (main photograph) p46; Shoe box storage (shoe box interior photographs) p78; Chunky tuna fishcakes p147; Quick kedgeree p152; Spicy chicken tortillas p154; Mango and coconut chicken p157
Stephen Hamilton/Gardeners' World: Potted topiary pp139-40
Scott Hawkins: Sweet chilli chicken p144; Red bean and tomato salsa p149; New potatoes with blue cheese and crispy bacon p159; Roast pepper salad p161
Alex James: Cooking for Special Occasions pp82-3; Decorating with Flowers pp108-109
Graham Kirk: Pies and pastries pp16-21
Jess Koppel: Unusual flower pots pp110-13; Candelabra ring pp134-5
Clive Nichols: Easy topiary p138
Alan Olley: Front cover, main photograph; The Big Easy pp142-3; The icing on the cake pp164-5
Debbie Patterson: Hop ring p115; Aromatic herbs pp134-7

STYLISTS
Angela Dukes: French tarts pp10-15; Gourmet gifts pp28-3; Drawstring bags pp62-5; Picture frames pp70-3; Papier mâché bowls pp74-7
Helen Payne: Pies and pastries pp16-21
Helen Trent: Gorgeous gateaux pp22-7; Perfect puddings pp34-9; Découpage plates pp42-5; Mosaic tabletop pp46-9; Canvas embroidery cushion pp50-3; Cross stitch picture pp54-7; Covered shelving pp58-61; Decorative lamps pp66-9; Shoe box storage pp78-81; Spring wedding pp84-91; Summer lunch party pp92-7; Christmas party pp102-7; Sweet chilli chicken p145; Chunky tuna fish cakes p146; Red bean and tomato salsa salad p148; Marinated olives with feta p150; Quick kedgeree p152; Spicy chicken tortillas p155; Mango and coconut chicken p156; New potatoes with blue cheese and crispy bacon p159; Roast pepper salad p160; Pecan grilled plums p162; Wedding cake pp166-71; Christmas tree cake pp184-7